Top 59
1st Editor   25
since   10

WHAT IS A MATURE MORALITY?

THE MACMILLAN COMPANY
NEW YORK · BOSTON · CHICAGO · DALLAS
ATLANTA · SAN FRANCISCO

MACMILLAN AND CO., Limited
LONDON · BOMBAY · CALCUTTA · MADRAS
MELBOURNE

THE MACMILLAN COMPANY
OF CANADA, Limited
TORONTO

WHAT IS A
MATURE MORALITY?

HAROLD H. TITUS

PROFESSOR OF PHILOSOPHY, DENISON UNIVERSITY,
GRANVILLE, OHIO

New York
THE MACMILLAN COMPANY
1943

To
MOTHER AND FATHER
on their
Fiftieth Wedding Anniversary

CONTENTS

CHAPTER   PAGE

I.   MORAL CONFUSION   I

II. THE BASIS OF A MORAL ORDER   24

III. ETHICS AND CHRISTIAN ETHICS   43

IV. MARKS OF A MATURE MORALITY   68

V.   COMPROMISE AND EXPERIMENTATION   106

VI. RELIGION, ETHICAL AND UNETHICAL   130

VII. IMPLICATONS FOR PRESENT-DAY SOCIETY   160

VIII. THE CRISIS AND OUR RESPONSIBILITY   192

     FOOTNOTES   219

     INDEX   225

WHAT IS A MATURE MORALITY?

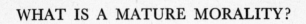

MORAL CONFUSION

M ANY THOUGHTFUL PERSONS in our time are speaking of the "decay" or "decline" or the "crisis" of Western civilization, or of the "end of an era." The older moorings and authorities seem to be disintegrating and people find it difficult to build new and stable foundations. Many of the standards and ideals that once were thought to be absolute and eternal are being questioned or disregarded. Many persons do not seem to know where to turn for guidance and direction. We are suffering not so much because of a lack of technology, of science, or even of general education, but because we have lost a sense of the meaning and goals of living. Unless we know the goals of living, the multiplication of means and techniques may merely hasten disaster. As nations and as persons, we are divided and face conflicts largely because of the ideas, the ideals, and the loyalties around which our lives are organized. When great loyalties exist today, they are too frequently of a divisive kind which set man against man. If we are to defeat the rising forces of barbarism, we shall need clear ideas and strong loyalties of the type which will unite men. Problems of morality and religion are among the most pressing problems of our time. The frontiers of our civilization are moral and spiritual rather than physical.

Change and Conflict

We live in a world that is changing rapidly. American society especially has been dynamic or fluid, subject to growth and to change. Recently those changes have come with a rush. One hundred years ago most men lived in a comparatively simple, agricultural, or rural society; today we live in a highly complex, interrelated, machine civilization. The fathers of most of us were born into a world that did not know the automobile, the radio, and the aeroplane.

While great changes have taken place in the physical or material conditions of living, our ideas, our customs, and our standards have also been changing. Twelve years ago if a man had walked down the street in any city in the United States carrying a bottle of beer and a ten-dollar gold piece, he could have been arrested for carrying the bottle of beer. Today he could be arrested for carrying the gold piece! Who would have thought, even five years ago, that we in America would ever consider the conscription of men and of materials in peace time as we did a year or two ago, or that in such a short time we would be engaged in a war which extends over the entire world and which will disturb civilization to its depths?

Since 1914 there is hardly a society in the world that has not undergone significant changes. In some parts of the world the changes have been more abrupt and thoroughgoing than in America. Old social orders have disappeared and new ones have taken their places. Fascism, communism, socialism, the co-operative societies, along with other movements, have been challenging some of the fundamental assumptions of the older social orders.

One of the oldest and most respected of living philosophers, Professor A. N. Whitehead, calls our attention to the shortening of the time-span of significant changes. Once these changes came slowly and covered a period longer than a human life. You and I live in the first period of history in which these changes tend to come within the lives of single individuals.

That, of course, creates new problems and difficulties. Lewis Mumford, in his *Faith For Living,* published in 1940, put this idea a little differently when he said that a thousand years separates 1940 from 1930.

The confusion and conflict in the international field is the most obvious at the present time. The world seems to be very near chaos with little regard for treaties, or the rights of individuals or of nations. During a single year, 1940–41, at least ten countries lost their national independence. The immorality of the present situation is seen in the fact that the nation, the race, or the group, is felt to be above ordinary ethical considerations. Men and women are appalled at the increase of cruelty and the decline of humanitarianism in our world.

The first World War came as a tremendous shock to a complacent and optimistic world. It was a major spiritual catastrophe which seemed to accentuate many of the very evils against which men claimed that they were fighting. Furthermore, it tended to destroy the cultural and industrial labors of generations of men and women and to leave cultural and economic maladjustment. It left a bitterness and a smouldering conflict that has again broken out into active warfare.

For a time, especially during the 1920's, men felt hopeful that the ideals of democracy, internationalism, and humanitarianism would prevail. There was much talk and some effort looking in the direction of disarmament and the building of instruments for the peaceful settlement of disputes. During the decade of the 1930's, however, fear, hatred, and the use of violence were on the increase. Allied to nationalism and irrationalism, they mark the rise of a new paganism. While the peoples of the world earnestly desired peace, they seemed forced to bend a large part of their energies to preparation for war. While the world, through the development of rapid means of communication and transportation had become a physical neighborhood, it was rent with suspicion, hatred, and a sense of great injustices.

Between the first World War and the war which started September, 1939, something had happened. In the first war men marched off amid shouting and singing and with a romantic patriotism. Since September, 1939, men have been marching in many lands, but the cheering and the enthusiasm are gone. They march off with a dull sense of duty. Whereas the first war came as a rude shock, when the new war started there was little optimism to destroy. This, in itself, however, may be a hopeful sign.

As a result of power politics, operating under the influence of national self-interest, a new anarchy is in evidence. Nations become aroused to action only when their national interests are at stake. If they still fight for ideals it seems to be only when those ideals are in line with their national interests. Men are worshipping political leaders, the state, a class, or a social and economic program. Things, institutions, and programs have thrust man rudely into the background.

When we turn from the international to the domestic scene, conflicts and confusion are still in evidence although they are likely to take a less violent form. During periods of war, national patriotism may cause them to lie dormant. Corresponding to national self-interest which leads to war, we have the doctrine of personal self-interest or the doctrine of the economic man. "The economic man" usually feels that he has a right to all the money and power he can accumulate. Corresponding to international rivalry we have the doctrine of "free competition" and business rivalry. Corresponding to the doctrine of absolute national sovereignty which leads nations to resist external control by a league or court or superstate, we have the doctrine of *laissez-faire* or individualism. International conflict is closely related to the domestic, economic, and political policies and practices of nations. However, these doctrines, and the practices which correspond to them, have been meeting opposition and facing restrictions in recent years.

Modern societies are marked by disputes between various functional groups. For example, industrial disputes have been, and are, widespread and fairly continuous. While the members of each group appeal to standards, it is difficult to find standards which are acceptable to all the groups concerned and which can be used as a basis for harmony. Employers may appeal to the rights of freedom of contract and of property, while the employees may appeal to the rights of a living wage, of security, and of collective bargaining. The reports of the Senate subcommittee on Violations of Free Speech and Rights of Labor will indicate to what extent these differences lead to an almost continuous struggle between employers and employees. Every now and then this struggle breaks into open industrial conflict. The evidence indicates that many corporations have been accustomed to plant spies in labor unions, to bribe union members, to use threats against men who are engaged in union activities, and to supply gas and other munitions to their own agents and to the police. On the other hand, the unions use methods of picketing and the strike to force recognition of the unions and to obtain better working conditions. While picketing and strikes are legal, their use can be greatly abused. Recent disclosures have shown that sometimes unions have used methods closely approaching those of the racketeer. They have sometimes shown little concern for the larger interests of the community.

If we examine the codes of conduct that have been adopted by the numerous business and professional groups, we find widely varying standards in operation. There is one standard for the business man, another for the doctor, another for the lawyer, and still a different one for the teacher. For the business man to operate on the basis of the profit motive or private gain is considered right, whereas the professional man is expected to accept the service motive and to ask first, not what he is going to make, but how he can help the person. For the doctor to build a private fortune by the use or the sale of some secret method or discovery that leads to the cure of disease or the alleviation of pain would be unprofessional. Yet in business a similar procedure is considered good business and the government gives aid through the patent office.

While the professions, as distinct from business, have adopted the service motive as their ideal, the code may protect the profession more than the public. George Bernard Shaw has called the doctor's code a "conspiracy against the public" because of the individual fee system with its abuses, such as the division of fees for the purpose of securing patients, and the protection of incompetent men within the profession. However, the doctors as a group have maintained fairly high standards and have retained more respect than some other professional groups. Today there is a controversy within and without the medical profession over the issues of group medicine, cooperative medicine, and state medicine.

As a man passes from group to group in society, he passes under different standards. Consequently, it is often difficult for him to make his life ethically consistent. One person may find that different standards are expected of him as he passes from home to church, to business, to club, to political activities, or as he goes to war. Even though he may be unconscious of it, the small boy may have three languages and three codes, one for the home, another for school, and still another for his gang activities. Later in life, as a man, he may find it difficult to bring the different segments of life under one standard.

A recent book in the field of business ethics points out that a man, in his business activities, may have three standards. First, there is the standard which he applies to his treatment of his customers, competitors, and those with whom he has dealings. Second, there is the standard which he expects them to follow when they are dealing with him. Finally, there is the standard by which he judges other people's treatment of their fellowmen. The following example is given: "A certain coal dealer, having made a great deal of money by selling coal in the conventional way, decided to branch out. The method he pursued was to go to small towns and propose to the sole or leading retailer to buy him out. The price offered was uniformly 50 per cent of the value of the plant. If the unfortunate victim of this program refused the offer, he was informed that the person in question would establish a business in the same town and would match every price set by the local dealer with one 20 per cent lower. The result was that our predatory adventurer accumulated by this and similar practices a large fortune. Instead of resting on his laurels he decided to become a national figure and invested most of his capital in an allied line. As soon as he was well under way the 'big business' organization dominating the industry made essentially the same proposition to him that he had made to scores of smaller dealers. He decided to fight rather than to surrender and finally retired from the field bereft of a large part of his wealth. Thereupon he called upon High Heaven to witness the injustice with which he had been treated. The men who had robbed him of his money were no better than common thieves and ought to be behind the bars." [1]

The prevalent standards and practices frequently have had tragic effects in the lives of men and women. Domestically, in the world's richest country, there has been near-starvation in the midst of plenty. Except for social relief, eight million families would have faced starvation. According to the chief executive of the nation, one-third of the nation has been "ill-fed, ill-clothed, and ill-housed." Before war conditions raised wages and the demand for workers, half of the population was living on incomes of $1250 or less, an amount which is not adequate for physical efficiency, health, and decency for the average family. The expression "poverty in the midst of plenty," so frequently heard in recent years, is a serious indictment of our social order. Why should the sharecroppers, the migrants, the slum-dwellers, the negroes, and other under-privileged groups be eager to preserve society as it is? Today defense needs and total war effort are temporarily helping to meet the problem. What the situation will be, after the sudden collapse of the defense industry, with a return of peace, startles one with its possible dangers. During a period in which the population has increased two and one-half times, the insanities have increased eleven times, jail population six times. Part of the unrest and revolt in the modern world is due to the fact that so many people have no stake in a society which shows such disregard of both men and materials and which produces so many warped and stunted lives.

Society is faced with numerous unsolved social problems and domestic disorders. A considerable part of these are due to the fact that society itself lacks a moral foundation. While moral and religious leaders may point out the need of good will, co-operation, and sharing, in actual practice society is organized around acquisitive self-interest and competitive rivalries. Is it any wonder that many persons, young and old, refuse to lead a double life or to leave themselves open to the charge of inconsistency or hypocrisy? They put religion and morality aside or reduce them to mere segments of life.

Is the confusion and conflict on the international and the domestic scenes a cause of, or a result of, personal perplexity and wrongdoing? Many persons are confused, discouraged, and unhappy. In part, it is because of what is going on in the world. There are so many things which they cannot reconcile with their conception of religion and of morality, or with their ideal of what ought to be. In part, it is because they have no great goals or loyalties around which their lives can be organized and integrated. They lack a cause, a devotion, a philosophy of life, which will give them poise and a sense of direction.

Recently a man said: "I am discouraged. All the ideals and values for which I have worked during recent years appear to be losing out and going into eclipse." The following experience reported by a contributor to *Harper's Magazine* seems to be somewhat common: "In the course of a few hours not long ago I heard a series of remarks worth quoting for their similarity. A business executive said, 'I am so uneasy about everything that I find it hard to make decisions.' A physician said, 'Nothing can induce me to part with the forty acres of land I own. Whatever happens in the next years I propose to eat.' A woman said, 'I adore my children, but lately I have caught myself almost wishing I had never brought them into the world.' Here were three intelligent people who were afraid and suffering acutely because of it. . . . People who have seemed tight-lipped and sufficient suddenly let fall a remark which startles one with the intensity of the apprehension it reveals. Less sturdy personalities are simply fleeing from reality into some form of mental disease." [2] We are told that half of the hospital beds in the United States are occupied by persons who are suffering from some sort of mental disorder.

A considerable part of the personal perplexity is due to the fact that many persons do not understand the nature of morality and its relation to life. On a number of occasions I have asked groups of adults as well as groups of young people to give their answers to the question, "Why is right right?" or,

"What is the basis of the distinction between right and wrong?" These groups have included church classes, classes in general adult education, and classes of fairly mature college students. The answers are so many and so varied that it is necessary to classify them under at least seven different headings. Since we shall have occasion to discuss these and related points, in later chapters, we shall do little more than mention them here.

Apart from those who say that they do not know or are uncertain about the distinction between right and wrong, the answers are likely to fall into the following classes: 1. *Personal preference.* Morality is a matter of private opinion and no one else should tell a person what he should or should not do. There are no standards which can be applied to all men. 2. *Customs, tradition, social approval,* or what is *legal.* "When in Rome do as the Romans do." In Japan it is wrong for a man and a woman to kiss in public; in Germany for a woman to use lipstick in public; in the United States to appear in "shorts" on the streets of some cities. What is legal in some states is illegal in others. South Carolina forbids absolute divorce for any reason, while some states grant divorces freely. In two states there are no illegitimate children, for the statutes declare that every child is the legitimate child of its natural parents. In some states the teaching of the theory of evolution is illegal; in most states it is legal. 3. *Conscience—"Let your conscience be your guide."* Conscience is the name for the restraining influences upon conduct which come from within. Since the dictates of conscience, even of conscientious Christians, differ widely, this standard is highly individualistic. While it is right to follow one's conscience, one's conscience is not always right. Our consciences often need training and redirecting, as we shall see. 4. *The Bible, the Church, the Will of God, or some religious authority.* Since there are between two hundred and three hundred religious denominations or sects in America, each one believing that it is nearer the right and the truth than most other groups, these standards do not lead to unity. Men both oppose and support personal participation in war on biblical and religious grounds. There can be no argument against the claim that it is right to do the Will of God, but how are we to discover in each case what is God's Will for us? There is no fixed body of moral precepts labelled "God's Will." Almost all peoples have attributed their moral code to their gods or to God. In the Bible, God is represented at an early time as commanding actions which later were thought to be wrong. We shall consider Christian ethics in chapter three. 5. *An appeal to nature or what is natural.* Down through history some men have appealed to natural law or to natural rights to support their basic convictions. There is a tendency today, however, for men to talk about human rights which may change from age to age. If some products of nature are good and others evil, then nature is not the only basis of our judgments of right and wrong. 6. *Happiness or personal pleasure.* While this view has been held by many persons, it is evident that one man's pleasure or displeasure seems to depend to a considerable extent upon his character and cultural development. 7. *Social welfare or the good of society.* If this means that acts are to be judged on the basis of their effect on persons, it may be accepted as a fairly adequate statement. That is right which is conducive to the well-being of men.

The answers given above to the question, "Why is right right?" would appear to indicate that the problem involves largely a difference of opinion. The trouble, however, may be much deeper. In writing about "This Pre-War Generation," Mortimer J. Adler says,[3] "The veterans of the last war had had 'illusions'; they had pledged themselves in the name of 'ideals.' They were a lost generation because they had lost something. But it would be incorrect to speak of the present generation as disillusioned or demoralized. They seem to have grown up without any allegiances that could be betrayed, without a moral philosophy to renounce." We shall discuss this moral skepticism in the following chapter.

Trends in Our Civilization

Modern man could stand the present confusion and disintegration better were it not for the fact that it has come upon him right at a time when he thought he was making great advances, and when he thought a better day was within clear sight. The contrast between the present and the recent past makes his present plight more painful. During the late nineteenth century, and during the first decade of the twentieth century, faith in man, in the meaning of life, in human intelligence, in progress, and in democracy were strong. Man was the crowning achievement of long periods of development and he was considered to be a child of God. Life had a meaning and a purpose as few persons would deny. Human intelligence had shown its marvelous powers in the achievements of science and in the reflections of philosophy. Men hoped that reason would be able to grapple with and to conquer most of the obstacles to man's welfare. There was, men thought, a growing moral consciousness. Faith in progress and democracy were naturally allied to these convictions.

Men held such convictions because they felt there was a secure basis for such a faith. Most of them believed in God, in the cosmos, in evolution, and in human intelligence. If some of them disbelieved in one or more of these bases, there were others which gave them hope. The Victorian Age thought of progress as inevitable. Knowledge, happiness, and power would grow "from more to more." Herbert Spencer could say that "Progress is not an accident but a necessity." Tennyson could assure us that "the thoughts of men are widened with the process of the suns."

Now, however, the old vision and hope, and the older sense of security, are gone. Men no longer have the same faith in man, in the meaning of life, in human intelligence, and in science. With the dimming of faith in God and in himself has gone his faith in democracy and in the inevitability of progress.

For some years I have been impressed by the number of books and articles that have said or taken for granted that we are in a period of decline. For example, toward the latter part of his book *No Compromise*, Melvin Rader says: "No one who has considered the evidence in the preceding chapters can doubt that we are living in a mad age . . . There has been a startling increase in superstition, in jingoism, Jew-baiting, violence, and warfare . . . Our delicately interdependent civilization may not be able to endure the very unequal rate of advancement between morals and mechanics; the entire pattern of our culture may at last be shattered. These statements are not unduly alarmist. They are just what wise men have been saying, and what even the most humble have been thinking." [4]

A few years ago, E. Stanley Jones wrote: ". . . The foundations of society are crumbling before our very eyes . . . As I go about the world I find men with the feeling that the Germans must have had when the Hindenburg line began to crumble." [5] Had this been written more recently he might have added: "Or as the French must have felt when the Maginot line gave way or was outflanked, or as the British must have felt when Singapore fell." In like manner, W. M. Horton says: "The fact is that civilization in the democratic nations is very badly disintegrated and cannot be saved without deep-going reconstruction, starting from a rediscovery of the Christian bases of democracy, and involving every aspect of life, from center to circumference." [6] One report on the Oxford Conference, a world conference of Christians in 1937, said: "A major emphasis in the deliberations of the Conference . . . was the disintegration of modern society, the collapse of standards." [7]

A few decades ago Oswald Spengler wrote a two-volume work called *The Decline of the West.* It was a prophecy of doom based on a study of the cultures of the past and of the trends in Western civilization. The first draft was written before the first World War, but the book was not actually published in Germany until after the war. Recently there has been a new interest in Spengler and a growing fear that he may be right. Let us consider his views briefly.

According to Spengler, cultures are like organisms: they live and die. They pass through the stages of childhood, youth, manhood, and old age, or through seed time and spring, summer's blossoming, autumnal fading, and winter's death. He examines the cultures of the past, such as the Egyptian, Chinese, Hindu, Classical Greek and Roman, and the Arabian, to show that there is a pattern of development.

Turning then to the West, he says that it is in its critical stage of decay, and he attempts to present the evidence. The decline of Western civilization begins with the industrial revolution and the invention of machines which lead to modernity and a decline of the human spirit. Great fortunes are built up and wealth increases, but simplicity and peace depart. The body develops and prospers, but the soul decays. Men leave the land for the cities which whirl with machines and are crowded with workers devoid of property, and a cultureless bourgeoisie or middle class groups. While distinction tends to pass to men of wealth, the business men never create, they merely accumulate and exchange; they are busy extracting money from other men's accounts to their own. The dictatorship of money is a sign of decay. Three or four great cities come to control the world. Imperial dictators seize the citadels of power. The population becomes sterile. Persons do not reproduce their kind. The reproduction of ignorance outruns the propagation of intelligence. There is increasing dependence. Religion and philosophy and science tend to crystallize into fixed forms. Life is fast and shallow.

Can we accept these views of Spengler? Is this what we face today? Are we destined to make up the backwash of a dying age? Before commenting on Spengler's views, I wish to mention a few other studies of a similar type and scope. Books on the philosophy of civilization have been multiplying at a rapid rate. With few, if any, exceptions, they agree with Spengler that our civilization is in a state of decay, at least in certain of its phases. They differ as to what can be done about it.

In his three-volume work, *Social and Cultural Dynamics,* P. A. Sorokin of Harvard University agrees with Spengler that our culture is in a very critical or dangerous state, and that in many phases it is declining rapidly. Life is becoming shallow with its emphasis upon quantity and its neglect of quality. "Not only the economic and political systems, but every important aspect of the life, organization, and culture of the Western society is included in the crisis. Its body and mind are sick and there is hardly a spot on its body which is not sore, nor any nervous fiber which functions soundly." [8] However, he rejects the four stages through which Spengler believed a culture must pass and says that our culture is not doomed to perish or even to decline. It is more likely to pass through a "grim transition" to a new phase.

Much the same problem and evidence is surveyed with even greater thoroughness by Arnold Toynbee, an English scholar, in his six-volume work, *A Study of History.* This is a philosophy of history written under the auspices of the Royal Institute of International Affairs. He agrees with Spengler that our Western civilization is rapidly declining, especially in certain of its phases. Out of twenty-six civilizations considered, only ten show any life today. Of these, two, the Polynesian and the Nomadic, are in their last agonies. Seven out of the other eight are either under threat of annihilation or assimilation by Western culture. They are the Orthodox Christendom of the Near East, Russian Orthodox Christendom, Islamic Society, Hindu Society, Far Eastern Society in China, Japanese Society, the Esquimaux Society. But Western civilization itself is in danger of losing its vitality and creative power. Civilizations break down when there is "a failure of creative power in the minority," a lack of leadership, and a "consequent loss of social unity."

Toynbee maintains that the decline in the West can be stopped. A time of crisis or a time of trouble has often jeopardized civilizations in the past with widely different results. Some societies have been crushed and have sunk into oblivion. Others, in going down, have given birth to vigorous new civilizations. Still others have met the challenge to their existence, and in the act of struggle have achieved a rebirth. The great advances come when danger or crises shatter men's composure without sapping their strength. If strength can be retained, the possibility of revival and advance is great.

Our Western civilization, according to Toynbee, needs a profound moral and spiritual transformation, if it is to survive. There must be less emphasis upon quantity, more upon quality; less regard for mere mechanical efficiency, more concern for aesthetic and moral sensitiveness. He believes that moral needs are now of first importance.

In *The Philosophy of Civilization* and *Out of My Life and*

Thought, Albert Schweitzer sees a possible retrogression represented by an intellectual and spiritual fatigue. It is his conviction that the catastrophe of civilization started from a breakdown of world-view. The essential element in civilization is the struggle to perfect the individual and society. Only a society which is striving after ethical ends can realize the blessings of material progress and eliminate the dangers which are likely to accompany such changes. He says: "To the question whether I am a pessimist or an optimist, I answer that my knowledge is pessimistic, but my willing and hoping are optimistic." [9] And again, "If men can be found who revolt against the spirit of thoughtlessness, and who are personalities sound enough and profound enough to let the ideals of ethical progress radiate from them as a force, there will start an activity of the spirit which will be strong enough to evoke a new mental and spiritual disposition in mankind." [10]

Interpretations like those of Toynbee and Schweitzer are in my opinion saner and nearer to the realities than that of Spengler. The latter erroneously thinks of cultures as organisms, and he overestimates the validity of analogy as a method of reasoning. There is not the inevitable life cycle in cultures that there is in organisms. He ignores the possibility of the rapid diffusion of the constructive forces as well as of the destructive forces in society. Moreover, there is a new fact in the modern world that makes us different from all past civilizations. We know the past, and we have methods of discovering trends such as no group of men have had in the past. Few, if any, knew at the time that Rome was declining. Today men know that something is wrong and they are fearful. That is a sign of encouragement in the present crisis. Today social ills can be discovered and controlled as never before, *if* we have the vision, the courage, and the will to do so. Part of the task of this book will be to discover the moral basis for revival.

Causes of the Present Confusion

The disorders of our age are deeper and more widespread than most persons realize. The causes are many and varied. They are involved and it is often difficult to say what is cause and what is effect. Human behavior may be viewed from many different points of view: physical, biological, social, moral, or religious, etc. There is a continuous interaction, and the different aspects of life may be separated only for purposes of analysis. No one point of view ordinarily exhausts a given event. May I suggest, however, that the following are important as causative factors in the present moral confusion:

First, the great social and industrial changes produced by the industrial revolution which began in the eighteenth century and expanded so rapidly in the nineteenth century. The industrial revolution has changed and is changing our world. It is still going on, unless one prefers to call the later developments the "technological revolution." The spread of machine techniques and modern science have not only changed man's ways of living, but they have revolutionized his thinking and his standard of values. Money and power have come to the fore as human incentives. Speed and noise have strained man's nerves and made deliberation or reflection more difficult. A separation between economics and ethics has led to conditions which are as uneconomic as they are immoral.

Second, a cause allied to the above has been the tendency to interpret human life, and culture, in mechanistic terms carried over uncritically from the physical sciences. Mechanistic conceptions may interpret quite adequately the fields of physics, chemistry, and the mechanical sciences. They are useful on the biological level, although even here there are new qualities or powers, such as growth, metabolism, reproduction, sensitivity, irritability, and the like, which cannot be completely explained in such terms. When we come to the human level, the physical and biological factors are not left behind, but there are new qualities and characteristics which set man off in a realm by himself. In addition to the qualities of the two former levels, man lives in a realm that is to some extent self-conscious, intelligent, moral, and spiritual. He has the power of reflective thinking or deliberation, of forming moral distinctions, and of judging not only what is, but what ought to be. Man has memory, imagination, ideas, ideals, and the power of creativity. He has all those powers and qualities which we associate with science, philosophy, art, and religion. To interpret man as if he were merely as other animals, as if he were merely chemical, or biological, or economic, or as if he could be interpreted adequately in terms of mechanism, is to ignore fundamental distinctions. Theories which interpret man as if he were without moral discernment or responsibility are in part responsible for the loss of the "Great Tradition" which interprets man as partaking of the divine and his life as in some sense meaningful and purposeful. The loss of this conviction is in part responsible for man's discouragement and loss of spirit.

Third, closely related to the tendency to emphasize the mechanistic sciences and man's animal nature is "the retreat from reason" or an attack upon the thinking man and upon rationality. Some students of contemporary life believe that a blind attack upon reason as a guide, an attack which fails to distinguish between the legitimate and the illegitimate uses of reason, is "What has produced the crisis in our civilization." [11] The exclusively empirical interpretations of knowledge tend to discredit reason and logic as sources of truth unless their results are verified by the sense organs. Men ought to accept, it is said, only that which we can see, hear, touch, smell, taste, or perceive through our senses. From another point of view, extreme specialization has led to a failure to place the results of human thinking at the disposal of social welfare. In the study of man, the Freudians, the Behaviorists, and others have minimized the place of reason and have stressed the unconscious, reflex arcs, and the like. In the interpretation of the universe, Schopenhauer and Nietzsche have had considerable influence. Schopenhauer stressed will or craving as the essence of all life. Nietzsche combined this view with Darwin's theory of natural selection, and it became the will to power or the struggle of life against life. The brave ruthless man is the ethical ideal. Fascism, by its glorification of sentiment, will, and action, and its lack of respect for intelligence and education, is in part an outcome of this retreat from rationality.

Fourth, war and the struggle between freedom and autocracy. The sharp struggle between the free spirit of man, represented by the democratic movement, and the autocratic and plutocratic forces, represented by industrial and financial monopoly, political nationalism, and dictatorship of the fascist type, has been a disruptive factor in our world. Some of the great pages of history tell of the struggles for liberty. The Renaissance saw the emancipation of the individual from rigid tradition. The revolutions of the seventeenth and eighteenth centuries were fought for the civil and political freedom and equality of the people. During the nineteenth century those objectives were fairly completely attained in many countries. The struggles of the twentieth century are centering chiefly around the drive on the part of the people for economic freedom and security under modern conditions and for the right of men to continue to think and to express their thoughts freely. The rise of totalitarian states abroad with their denial of freedom has sharpened the struggle and made this one of the most important, as well as one of the most disturbing, issues in the modern world. Due to the gravity of the fascist menace and its direct attack against the foundations of our civilization, fascist ethics will be considered briefly in the next chapter.

Instead of the revolutionary changes of our time being merely a part of the war, I am suggesting that the war is only one phase, the violent stage, of a revolution which to a considerable extent is world wide. Future historians may view both the first World War and the present conflict as parts of great revolutionary changes which were taking place during the twentieth century. The war, however, is greatly accelerating the pace of change and the extent of its destructiveness.

The shattering effects of this second World War in which we are engaged may be much greater than those of the World War 1914–1918. Free men are coming more and more to recognize that after victory is won for the democratic forces, we must build a world in which war is eliminated, or war will eventually crush our finest ideals and our civilization. While the cultural and industrial labors of men and women for generations may be destroyed in time of war, the defilement of the human spirit may be even greater.

Fifth, two problems within the realm of morality itself have contributed to the present moral confusion. The first is the contention of the ethical relativists: that there are no universal or objective standards which can be applied to human conduct and group behavior. We shall discuss this attack upon morality in the chapter on The Basis of a Moral Order. The second problem is due to our failure to bring our moral principles up to date.

The failure to apply even our tested and accepted principles of morality to our modern ways of living is a serious handicap. In the main we have been trying to run a complex, machine civilization with the moral outlook of an earlier age. Many of our moral codes and traditions were formulated in a simple society dominated by intimate personal relations. Such a society is characterized by what the sociologists call primary group relationships, where people meet freely and informally in work and at play. Today, however, we live in a society dominated by formal, impersonal relations or by complex groups and institutions. Such a society is dominated by secondary groups. Men tend to meet for a specific purpose and in one segment of life only. Interdependence is the order of the day and long range immorality is possible. A man's acts may affect others whom he has never seen. Codes based on a pastoral or an agricultural order may seem remote to urban minds.

Man's moral progress has not kept pace with his rapid material, technological, and intellectual progress, and consequently his culture and his civilization are in danger. Man has fairly successfully conquered and controlled nature; will he be able to understand and to control himself? Is man any happier or any wiser because his voice can reach across the continent or across the ocean? Is he any better because he can travel ten or twenty times as fast as his grandfather could when he was a boy? Speed and power are means that can be used for many ends. A civilization depends upon its sense of values and not upon technical progress alone.

A good case could probably be made for the view that the present world situation, with its conflicts and tensions, is due in large part to a breakdown in moral standards, or at least to a failure to apply those standards to modern life. There has been no lack in the development of science or technology, nor even of general knowledge. Men are coming more and more to realize that these things can be used to destroy man, just as they can be used to promote human welfare. The standards, the loyalties, the moral ideas under which a people live are basic.

Finally, a loss of religious passion and a separation of religion from morality, from science, and from everyday life have brought about moral confusion. Religion, too, has undergone disintegration and, in many parts of the world, it has declined in prestige or respect. When it ceases to enter into all aspects of life, it is in danger of being eliminated entirely. Religion is the vital warmth, the conviction of the worth of life, the will to live nobly, which is the basis of society. When this wanes, or dies, men tend to lose faith in the meaning and significance of life. In the past, civilizations have decayed because of a loss of religious passion that provided the driving force to high endeavor. In later chapters we shall consider further the relation between morality and religion.

While it is evident that there is widespread confusion and uncertainty, the present crisis appears to be caused not by great natural evils which are beyond man's control, but by selfishness, ignorance and lack of insight, divisive loyalties, and social change. His greatest dangers are not such obstacles as glaciers, earthquakes, or prolonged droughts, but personal and social problems which are to some extent within his power to change. The resources for revival are at hand and there is hope in the fact that many men are concerned about the disorders of their lives and of their world.

There seems to be no inevitability in human affairs except as men and women accept certain conditions as inevitable. They live in a world that can be made better than it is. There are great redemptive as well as demonic forces near at hand. The pressing need is for men to see the issues more clearly and to awaken to the meaning and possibilities of human existence. Today men are either confused and baffled, or they are reorganizing their values and setting out to make these values realities in human affairs.

CHAPTER II

THE BASIS OF A MORAL ORDER

ORALITY IS AN OBSERVANCE of the laws of wholesome living. Some persons appear to believe that it is mere obedience to artificial conventions, a shallow desire for "respectability," or that it originated with the Puritans of Massachusetts or the English under Queen Victoria! There are, however, two serious threats to morality that we need to consider. In the preceding chapter, we pointed out that morality is being undermined from two directions: by a rising fascism which glorifies action and which denies the fundamental values upon which our civilization has been built; and, by ethical relativism, and related points of view, which claim that no moral judgments have objective validity. After a brief examination of these movements and their criticisms of contemporary morality, we shall inquire into the basis of genuine ethical standards.

Fascist Morality

During recent decades there has arisen a way of life or an outlook, known as fascism or totalitarianism, that is a denial not only of Christian ethics but of the fundamental tenets upon which Western civilization has been built. I shall use the term "fascism" to include not only the regime in Italy since Mussolini's "March on Rome" in 1922, but also National Socialism in Germany and movements of a similar nature elsewhere. What is fascism? I shall make six statements, no one of which is complete in and of itself, but when these statements are put together I think they present a fairly complete idea of fascism, its outlook, and its spirit.

In the first place, fascism is extreme statism or extreme nationalism. The state is absolute. It is superior to all individuals and groups, whether those groups are political, civil, economic, educational, scientific, religious, or what not. Consequently the movement is called totalitarianism. Fascism is the absolute sovereignty of the state, the conception of the state as power. As Mussolini has said, "For the fascists . . . all is in the state and nothing human or spiritual exists and much less has any value outside the state." The highest duty then is to serve the state. This totalitarian conception of the state stands in sharp contrast to the traditional American ideal, an ideal "that governments derive their just powers from the consent of the governed," and that government is an instrument for the promotion of the life, liberty, and happiness of the individual citizen. It is also opposed to the Christian ethical ideal. To make the state absolute is as immoral as it is dangerous.

In the second place, because of this glorification of the state as an instrument of power, fascism is militaristic and justifies the use of violence and coercion both at home and abroad. Consequently, we have seen in fascism a repudiation of the ideal of peace and brotherhood, of internationalism, and of humanitarianism. In *Mein Kampf*, Hitler speaks of humanitarianism as a compound of stupidity, cowardice, and arrogance, and says that ". . . in constant struggle mankind has become great—in eternal peace, it must perish." This side of fascism is too well known to need elaboration. There is also violence in domestic life. Opposition has been crushed by the use of the whipping post, imprisonment, concentration camps, and even death purges. One must conform or starve or be eliminated. Mussolini has said, "Violence today has become the best condition of real health for a people. For the present esthetic of filthy lucre we oppose an 'esthetic of violence and blood'." Gentile, one of the Italian philosophers, who has not fled the country, but is helping to build up the ideology of the movement, has said, "Cruelty enjoined by the state becomes holy violence."

In the third place, fascism, negatively, is a complete repudiation of the ideals of democracy and freedom, while positively it accepts dictatorship as the ideal. Fascists reject the ideals of liberty, equality, and fraternity. Instead of the formula "society for individuals," they substitute "the individual for society." More positively, dictatorship is the ideal. There is one leader, the duce, the fuehrer, and his will is supreme. Power flows from the top down. The will or authority of the leader is carried out by one party which tolerates no opposition. We have in fascism this cult of the leader, and rule not by discussion and ballots but by decrees and bullets.

In the fourth place, on its economic side, fascism is the ideal of the corporative state, a state which makes possible a form of economic planning under which employers and workers are supervised servants of the state. The state has final jurisdiction over wages, prices, and profits. Fascism thus accepts the class formation of society but permits no open conflicts to occur within society.

In the fifth place, fascism is traditionalism. It appeals to the past and builds on the myths of cultural and racial superiority. In this sense, it is really a new tribalism. The emphasis on racial purity and racial superiority leads to attacks on other peoples as inferior, and in Germany it has led to especially bitter attacks against the Jews.

In the sixth place, fascism is irrationalism which expresses itself, on one side, in opportunism and, on the other side, in an anti-intellectualism. Once, when asked regarding his program,

Mussolini replied, "Our program is simple. We wish to govern Italy." The tactics of opportunism as a bid for power were later rationalized and defended. Mussolini has said, "We play on all the strings from violence to religion, from art to politics." Again, fascism is part of the movement in the modern world known as "the retreat from reason." There is an emphasis upon sentiment and feeling, rather than upon intellect, upon will and action rather than reason. "We think with our blood" is a phrase which is frequently heard in the fascist countries today.

The philosophy which is embodied in democracy, and which underlies modern science, is objective and enquiring. It relies on persuasion and logical processes and appeals to facts to convince men. It rejects authority, propaganda, and ignorance, and asks for evidence, education, and knowledge. Not so fascism, which is irrationalism. Fascism stresses authority, obedience, and the use of methods of propaganda and force. It has contempt for the intelligence of the ordinary man, and especially keen contempt for the intelligence of women.

So much for the points on which German and Italian fascists agree. German fascism, or Nazism, differs mainly in being a more aggressive and a more fully developed form of fascism. It is more ruthless, both in its foreign and in its domestic policies. Again, German fascism places greater emphasis upon blood and race than does Italian fascism. This statement of fascist ideology which I have outlined would fairly closely describe the outlook of the military clique in Japan, except that in Japan the person of the Emperor is held in highest devotion.

To a considerable extent an exposition of the tenets of fascism on the basis of official statements and acknowledged practices is sufficient to condemn this movement for those in whom human sympathy and reason have not been blotted out. Fascism is an opportunism and a naked self-assertion of power which is a denial of ethics. The glorification of the state, of the race, of militarism, and of war are highly dangerous to human welfare and to civilization. How can men justify the use of secret police, espionage, brutality, and murder, except on the basis of their own warped desire for power, and the view that any means are justified to gain their ends?

Fascism, with its denial of the claims of the person and of intelligence, runs counter to some of the main trends in the evolution of morality. It is also a direct challenge to the Christian doctrine of the Fatherhood of God. Consequently, we are not surprised to hear that there has been talk in Germany of restoring the older Nordic tribal gods for the purpose of stimulating nationalism.

The fascists have perverted education and culture to their own ends. They have forced men to become slavishly responsive to authority rather than free and reflective moral agents. If fascism has an ethics in any real sense of the word, it is a crude tribal code which can lead only to anarchy in the modern world.

Fascism is dynamism without any real values. Hermann Rauschning is probably right when he speaks of fascism as "the voice of destruction" and "the revolution of Nihilism." He quotes Hitler as saying: "I am the greatest liberator of humanity from the gross degrading superstition of Christianity." Fascism is a declaration of war against human personality, the Christian ethics, and a rational order of society and progress.

At this point someone may raise the question as to why we have criticised fascism and have omitted communism. Are they not equally serious challenges to Western civilization and to Christian ethics? My reply is, first, that I am not aiming to discuss all the rival social ideologies, and secondly, that communism does not present the same immediate threat. The fascists have used tyrannical methods and they defend them. They repudiate freedom, democracy, and humanitarianism even as ideals. The communists have used similar methods but they do not idealize them. The dictatorship of the proletariat is, in theory, a transitional period. Freedom, equality, democracy are to be achieved in the final stage of communism and are accepted as ideals. While this final stage of "pure communism" may never arrive, there is in communism an internal basis for criticism and reform of the movement. Fascism, I believe, is more definitely anti-Western and anti-Christian than is communism. One can make this statement and still repudiate the extreme economic interpretation of history, the dictatorship, brutality, and the atheism of many communist leaders.

Ethical Relativism

The moral confusion of our time has also been increased by the view that morality is subjective, and that there are no objectively real moral standards. Values, it is claimed, are relative to the circumstances, to the time and the place of their appearance, and to the human mind. There are, therefore, no common standards among men, since whatever an individual or a social group thinks good is good. The opinion or taste of one man or group is as good as that of any other. This view that the rightness of an act and the goodness of a person or an object depend upon the interpretation or point of view of some individual or group toward them, and hence may vary from person to person, is known as ethical relativism. If you differ with your friend, he may remark, "Oh, that is only what you think." If he is more sophisticated, he may remark with Shakespeare, "There's nothing either good or bad, but thinking makes it so."

In an article entitled "Undergraduates and the War," written in 1940, Paul P. Cram pointed out that a considerable portion of young people did not see any moral issue involved in the international conflict or its outcome and resented the implication that there was one. He quotes one student as saying: "I won't go into the state of my morals, but in connection with this war it seems to me that morals are out of the question. In college, I studied some psychology, and the first lesson I learned was that there was no right or wrong to human behavior." [1] Some of the teachers of these undergraduates may have been logical positivists who take the position that ethical statements do not refer to any objective facts, but express merely the feelings and emotions of men. Moral judgments exist, it is true, but they are neither true nor false. There are no true principles of morality because there are no objective standards.

On the above basis, we cannot prove that one act is better than another, that one standard is superior to another, or that the principles underlying Western civilization are any better than those underlying totalitarianism. All we can say is that we prefer one to the other. The ethical relativists do not merely state that what some people *think* right in one place is thought by others to be wrong at some other place. Anyone would have to admit that much. They claim that what *is* right at one place is wrong at another place because there are no universal objective standards beyond human thinking and feeling.

A detailed examination of all the arguments for moral relativity would carry us too far afield. They are built on the assumption of a strict naturalism and take two lines of attack. First, they attack absolutism and authoritarianism in the realm of morals. They show that morality is relative to human needs, and then go on to assert that it is impossible to find the basis for a universally valid moral law. That morality is relative to human needs can be demonstrated; that it is not possible to find the basis for a moral law that is applicable to all men is probably false, as we shall see.

The second argument for moral relativity is based on the great variety of moral codes and practices found existing side by side in the world. Anthropologists and other students of man, past and present, have searched the early records of man. They have visited the jungles and deserts of Africa, the steppes and mountains of Asia, the islands of the Seven Seas, as well as various modern "civilizations," and they have disclosed countless examples of queer, bizarre, and contradictory practices. They may claim, with Westermarck, that moral ideas are based upon emotions, upon feelings of approval (admiration), and disapproval (resentment), which are rather capricious. They may quote Sumner [2] to the effect that moral ideas come from customs, and that the *mores* can make anything right or wrong. They may assert that moral ideas are based upon both emotions and customs.

Another argument for moral relativity is based on the views of the radical empiricists who hold that no word has real or cognitive meaning unless the thing to which it refers can be directly experienced. Now morality means what men ought to do. Since we can only experience what *is*, and not what *ought* to be, the word "ought" is meaningless and morality collapses. For those interested in this argument and its criticism, an excellent discussion will be found in *The Concept of Morals* by W. T. Stace.[3]

The case for moral objectivity, and against moral relativity, stands on two main considerations; one practical, or in the realm of moral conduct, the other intellectual, or in the realm of ethical standards. In the first place, if men come really to believe that morals are purely relative and subjective, so that one action is as good as another, it will make chaos of our moral, cultural, and spiritual lives. If one standard has nothing significant to commend it over another standard, why struggle to maintain a "higher" standard? Why not take the easiest way out of all circumstances? Skepticism, despair, and complete demoralization are likely to be the result, unless the person has already firmly established habits.

At this point, the moral relativist is likely to tell us that we can and ought to judge a person by the standards which he accepts, or by the standards of his group. But how can one ever know what is the moral standard of a group, since there are likely to be differences of opinion among the members of any group? Is it to be the majority? In that case, were all the reformers of the past mistaken? Is it some minority, and, if so, how select the right minority? If I wish to compare two persons I can never be sure whether they belong to the same group and accept the same standards. Then, too, most persons belong to many groups. The result is that each individual is bound by no standard except his own, and no one ought to question his conduct. If we cannot deny to any group the right to have its own standards, it is questionable if we can deny the same right to the individual.

In the second place, if all ethical standards are subjective and relative, morality itself becomes meaningless. If men have no common and universal standards which can be applied, it is foolish to make comparisons between persons and groups, to hold the idea of moral progress, or to encourage people to strive for higher ideals and a better world. Since what people think right is actually right for them, judgments of right and wrong merely express the conceit and egotism of the person making the judgment. This position, when carried to its logical conclusion, results in spiritual chaos and the collapse of all effective and intelligent standards of conduct.

In justice to the contentions of the relativists and skeptics, we shall have to admit that moral ideas and customs have changed from age to age and from place to place, and that morality has grown out of human needs and desires. Conscience is a product of individual and social experience and likewise undergoes change. The Hebrew and Christian Bibles present a picture of changing ideals and practices, or of a developing moral life. The history of Christian ethics is a record of change within a more stable frame of reference. Morals are relative to human needs and do change through human experience. The rejection of ethical absolutism and authoritarianism, however, does not prove the contentions of the ethical relativists, nor imply that there is no objective code of morality applicable to all men. Recent additional evidence of the great variety of moral codes and practices among different tribes and peoples has added nothing new.

I believe that it can be shown that questions of right and wrong are not mere matters of opinion, but questions of fact. A right action is not made right because some person or a community thinks it right or approves it. An act is right if it is the sort of act that has good results. Whether a person or a group recognizes it as right is quite secondary. We judge a thing good which is good for something. What that something is we shall have to consider more in detail later on. Suffice it to say here that conduct, intelligently appraised as good, is conducive to the welfare of persons or results in some gain in the total realization of life.

The Nature of Morality

In the light of these repudiations of morality by the fascist, on the one hand, and by the relativists and subjectivists, on the other hand, we are forced to examine the basis of moral obligation. Why live a moral life? Why be good? Morality, as we have seen, is an attempt to discover and to live the good life which is the healthy, the happy, the satisfactory, the full life. This life must be lived in the midst of present conditions and will depend upon the nature of persons or of man as well as upon the nature of the world in which men live. Human attitudes and actions must align themselves with the basic structure and processes of the universe, or life will certainly end in failure. Morality, like man's body, his language, and his institutions, has developed from meager beginnings. As experience, knowledge, and the power of reflection have expanded, the degree of human freedom has enlarged, and the requirements of personal and social welfare have tended to be taken more and more into account.

Running through all life there is the ever present will-to-live. This is a fundamental fact which cannot be denied. It is found all through the sub-human species of life, as well as on the human level. The will-to-live is everywhere, universal, persistent. In every living thing, plant, animal, man, there is a striving toward the expansion and fulfillment of its being. Wherever there is life there are conditions which must be met.

In the animal realm, what is right for the animal, what it ought to do, how it ought to live—the temperature, food, shelter, exercise, or its behavior—are settled by its animal nature. Nearly all of its actions are directed to the attainment of the good or the better and an effort to avoid the bad or the worse. The lion needs meat rather than nuts which would be good for the squirrel. The horse needs grass or hay and oats. The "rules of living" or the rules of health for the animal depend upon its anatomical and physiological structure or nature and upon its habitat or environment.

When we come to the life of man, we shall find that his conduct is also prescribed for him by his nature. His nature, however, is much more complicated and he has new powers

and capabilities, including some conscious freedom of choice.
If he lives this way he continues to live: if he lives that way,
life is decreased or ceases altogether. If man consents to live
he is valuing life to some extent.

> No churchyard is so handsome anywhere
> As will straight move one to be buried there.[4]

No man can live without acting, and when he acts he is
forced to make choices between the right and the wrong, the
good and the bad. No life is possible without making numerous
decisions, some of which may be trivial, but many of which
are of the utmost importance. Some of these decisions may
affect his entire life. Some acts are practically universally
disapproved among men, other acts receive widespread approval. Between the two are usually others which are subjects
for discussion and controversy. This problem of human conduct which has been so persistent throughout history has taken
on the name "morality." Consciously or unconsciously men
have been trying to discover the kind of life which is most
worth living. Elemental in human consciousness is this conviction that life is worth preserving. It may be expressed as "self-
preservation is the first law of life," or it may be expressed on
a higher plane as a supreme concern for all men.

Consider first the physical level of human existence. In order
to live man must meet certain conditions of temperature, air,
sunshine, and the like. Man must eat. Some things are good to
eat, and some things are not. "Eat some green vegetables,"
and "Do not eat toadstools" are demands he will do well to
obey. Man must also drink, sleep, exercise, and meet a host of
other demands if he is to live well. Apparently anger, fear, and
jealousy produce poison in the body as well as disrupt social
relations, while love, good will, and contentment make for
health. With increase of knowledge in medicine, and in the

sciences in general, man is able to live a more adequate and satisfactory physical and social existence.

Recent studies have made clear that some physical and biological factors make the development of a high moral character difficult and they help to explain some instances of failure and wrongdoing. Depressing or unfavorable climatic conditions, constitutional inferiority, organic defects, and the like are important here. If this is true then a part of our duty will be to irrigate deserts, to clear swamps, to install sanitary devices, to eliminate fatigue, to help cure diseases and defects that can be treated. These physical and biological demands are not merely emotional and subjective. They impose duties upon us which are objective and to a considerable extent universal.

Consider next the social level of existence. Man must associate with his fellows in numerous ways and there are equally numerous social demands (duties) that must be recognized. If men are to live together harmoniously, they must have regard for the desires, the feelings, and the needs of each other. In every aspect of life man is dependent upon his fellows. He needs to co-operate with others for protection against enemies, for his food and shelter, and for the establishment of the family, the school, and the state. If he is to live well he soon discovers that "We are members one of another."

Human conduct is never the result of environmental conditions alone, or of human traits alone. It is always the result of the interaction of the individual and his environment. Social groups are among the most important elements in that environment. Out of this social interaction folkways, mores, and institutional practices develop. With the growth of society, regulations have expressed themselves outwardly in custom, law, and in written codes of various kinds. Inwardly they have expressed themselves in a sense of duty, in satisfaction and dissatisfaction, and in shame and remorse. While moral standards have varied widely in the past, as knowledge and experience grow and expand, the requirements of human welfare are more and more taken into account. There are right and wrong ways of treating one's parents, one's children, one's husband or wife, and one's friends. There are right and wrong ways of caring for the sick, of playing games, of conducting a business.

Among all peoples, ancient and modern, the power of custom has been strong. An individual is born into a group which is a going concern with ways of thinking, feeling, and acting. What is custom in the group tends to become habit in the individual. Customs ordinarily arise from the needs of life, under certain conditions, and they are passed along and become powerful societal forces. We tend to feel a sense of obligation to respect them. They may, however, grow up under all sorts of irrational influences including chance, superstitions, and historical incidents and accidents, as well as under the pressure of human needs and through reflection. Customs vary according to the different climatic, geographical, biological, psychological, and social conditions under which men live. Changes come when strain appears, through conflicts, or through the criticisms of exceptional men. A moral system under which standards are determined almost exclusively by custom would be called "customary morality." It is not a mature stage of human development. An important difference between primitive and modern men is that modern men are more free to examine critically the customs of their day and to modify them in the light of experience and reflection. When customs are valuable they should be retained and supported. While we need to respect the feelings, traditions, and reverences of others, to take custom as the standard is to submerge the individual in the group and to stifle progress.

While psychologists, sociologists, and others who have studied man's nature do not always agree in their analysis and terminology, it is evident that there are basic human urges and desires which express themselves in much the same way wherever men are found. Unselfishness, friendship, honesty or integrity, self-control, courage are almost universally approved. Selfishness, treachery, murder, stealing, lying, and the like, are almost universally condemned. Here again the demand is so to live that you increase life. I can be happy only if I am concerned about the happiness of my fellows.

Here are two men, one of whom is affectionate, kind, honest, unselfish, tolerant, and self-disciplined; the other is callous, cruel, dishonest, selfish, intolerant, and sensuous. The judgment that one of them is a good man and the other a bad man is not an arbitrary, artificial, nor a merely subjective evaluation. Moral judgments which are based on man's entire nature ought to possess the same authority as the rules of health which rest on the narrower basis of man's physical nature.

On the levels of mind and spirit, which cannot be sharply separated from the social, there are also demands which man must meet. There is an almost universal human belief, expressed in the great religions and ethical systems of the world, that the satisfactions of the mind and spirit are more noble or higher than the satisfactions which pertain to the body or flesh alone. Even in the ethical systems that stress happiness as the goal of life, it is usually recognized that the satisfactions of the mind in science, art, philosophy, and religion yield a truer and more lasting happiness.

The classical Greeks were the first to stress the rationality of man and the view that his conduct should be guided by this rationality. Reason, they believed, was what distinguished and separated man from all other animals. Reason ought to be in control over the emotions and the appetites. To be reasonable was to be moderate. Plato, especially, made much of the notion of "proper function." Just as each of the parts of the body has its proper function which can be observed in the normal healthy person, so each of the elements of the personality likewise has its proper function. Just as the proper function of the heart is to pump blood through the body system, so it is the proper function of reason to rule. In man, reason ought to be in control and to guide human conduct because only in this way can he lead a satisfactory life. This conviction, first emphasized by the early Greeks, accepted by Christian thinkers, but not stressed as much as unselfishness, is one of the basic beliefs upon which our civilization rests.

To consider all the demands which reason or intelligence makes upon human life would carry us too far afield and would tend to cover the whole areas of science and philosophy. One thing, however, does need to be mentioned here. A demand of intelligence is for consistency in one's thinking and living. Consistency, in turn, means the living of one's life on the basis of principles. Logical consistency means conformity to the established principles of human thinking. Factual consistency means a recognition of the nature of the world in which we live. The stage of reflective morality is not reached until men formulate moral judgments on the basis of a reflective evaluation of principles and a careful examination of facts in their relation to human welfare. No person can live a satisfactory life who has not set up for himself some scale of values. Ethics attempts to stimulate the moral sense in man, to discover the true values of life, and to inspire men to join in the quest for these values.

Some persons would say that "morality is just being intelligent." There is some truth in this statement if we take intelligence as wisdom in the widest sense. Yet we know that knowledge alone, in the ordinary sense, is not enough. Clever men may be vicious. Knowledge may be used to destroy civilization as well as to help save it. Too frequently knowledge and intelligence have been thought of as ends-in-themselves, and they have been divorced from high human purposes. With all of our great progress in knowledge in recent decades, it is doubtful whether there has been a corresponding progress in morality. Some men are better for their intellectual achievements and some are worse. While intelligence and knowledge are essential ingredients of a high morality, they are not the only qualifications.

Man is by nature a being with emotions and feelings that must be developed and expressed or he is a warped soul. Love, hatred, fear, anger, and the like are contagious and tend to flow from person to person. This can be observed in all normal social situations but it is especially evident in all of those occasions like audiences and group gatherings where we receive stimulation through contact as well as through sight and sound. This psychological fact of sympathy is the basis of the Christian ideal of love, unselfishness, selflessness, altruism, or self-sacrifice. Sympathy is the principle by which the barriers between persons are broken down and communication is established. In the light of this fact it is interesting to note that all of the great ethical systems and moral codes which have stood the test of human experience for long periods have stressed unselfishness as the essence of morality and have condemned selfishness. The statement of Jesus: "Do unto others as you would that they should do unto you" is accepted by Christians as the very heart of morality. We shall discuss this ideal in another chapter.

Up to this point in our discussion of the basis of morality we have confined ourselves to strictly humanistic considerations. The good life is valuable in its own right, or for its own sake. When men cut themselves off from cosmic support or relinquish belief in God, they do not necessarily become immoral or vicious. The more immediate result is likely to be a lowered enthusiasm about life or a lack of morale. However, what man ought to do and to be depends upon what man is and upon his place in the universe. Ethical questions cannot be separated from questions as to the nature of the universe, the purpose and meaning of things, and other questions of religion. Ethics alone cannot decide such questions; yet the way they are answered will have a profound effect upon ethical theories and moral practice. Such answers will affect his spirit and outlook.

Man can gain support for his highest endeavors. There exists in the universe a process, a *nisus,* a creativity that makes for truth, beauty, and goodness. If man is to realize the good life and the fulfillment of his aspirations, he must intelligently and co-operatively relate himself to that in the universe which is "life-giving, truth-revealing, beauty-making, personality-producing." The creative urges within man would appear to be inherited from the universe which has produced him. They seem to be man's half-conscious realization of his own inherent possibilities. Those who deny the possibility of superhuman support for man in his quest for the good life base their views upon one or both of two assumptions. One is that the universe does not have meaning, nor value, nor intelligence in its structure and, therefore, if one uses such terms he is of necessity committing the fallacy of wishful thinking. The other is that the interpretations of the objective sciences are the only valid interpretations and that they are final and complete. Both of these assumptions are open to serious question, and many thoughtful persons reject them. I have briefly examined them elsewhere.[5]

Dr. W. E. Hocking has said: "It is becoming slowly recognized that where obligation or duty exists, there must be some object fit for that feeling: there can be no obligation to the lifeless, nor to the inanimate, nor to the morally blind. If the cosmos conveys to me a sense of moral demand, the term 'God' begins to acquire a core of meaning no longer repellent to the scientific consciousness." [6]

While admitting that he cannot give absolute proof to the skeptic, the Christian is one who believes that human personality is an enduring manifestation of an eternal spiritual order; that the universe is governed at heart by intelligence, good will, and moral purpose; that personal fellowship between man and God is possible and essential for the fulfillment of life's deepest meaning and significance; and that in the personality of Jesus men have the most adequate expression in human form of the moral good will which is needed for personal and social redemption.

CHAPTER III

ETHICS AND CHRISTIAN ETHICS

FROM TIME IMMEMORIAL men have formed codes of conduct to guide them in facing the problems and decisions of life. Some of the best of these codes have come down to us. While conditions of life have changed, and while the codes and the conduct of men have had to be adapted to new situations, nevertheless agreements, understandings, principles of behavior have remained. Much the same process of development has taken place among all the peoples of the earth. In Western civilization, Christianity has played a central part in the development of morality. In this chapter, therefore, we shall examine Christian ethics and its relation to ethics and morality in general.

Is there a "Christian ethics" or a "Christian morality" which is distinct from ethics and morality in general? A great many persons certainly feel that there is an outlook on life and an ethics or a morality which is peculiarly Christian. Is there a Christian mathematics or a Christian chemistry distinct from mathematics or from chemistry in general? In the latter case most educated persons would deny any difference. Mathematics may be true or false, but hardly Christian or unchristian. There appears to be one way of arriving at the truth of chemistry, and that is by observation and experimentation. Does the same thing apply to the principles of ethics and to moral codes? Are they merely true or false, reasonable or unreasonable, socially beneficial or detrimental?

There are problems, however, which face men in the field of values or in the normative studies, which are different from those in a formal science like mathematics or a descriptive science like chemistry. In the field of morality we are dealing with issues that are more personal and that involve the fundamental life attitudes and philosophies of men. Even more important than correct knowledge of the means and techniques to attain what we want are the goals or ends of living which we are seeking, since these are the very growing points of our experience. Before asking what is the distinctive thing about Christian ethics, let us look briefly at the development of ethics in general, then at the development of Christian ethics. This will help us in answering our questions.

The Development of Morality and Ethics

Our morals, like our bodies, our language, and our social institutions are the products of long periods of development. We shall have to resist the temptation to trace this story in some detail. From the very earliest times men have found it necessary, for the welfare of the group, to agree upon certain principles and practices and to require adherence from the members of the group. In primitive times the individual was almost completely submerged in the customs of the group. A man's rights and responsibilities were fairly definitely fixed by the group of which he was a member. In a stable environment this tended to keep the average man in line, but it also held back the exceptional man who otherwise might have forged ahead to new and better ways of doing things. The weakness of customary morality is that it tends toward social stagnation and formalism. It does not provide for criticism of existing institutions and practices or for revision under changing conditions.

With the growth of society, standards of conduct tend to express themselves outwardly in law and inwardly in conscience, as we have seen. The decrees of a ruler or of some law-making body take their place along with customs in the conduct of affairs. These laws may simply crystallize existing customs or they may change them. Conflicts may arise between customs, or between laws, or between a custom and a law. Such conflicts may lead men to search for some principle or standard of judgment. They may come to appeal to the feeling which they have that some things ought to be done. There is an inner law, a sense of obligation, which must be obeyed. This sense of moral obligation is called conscience.

The appeal to the conscience of the individual is not likely to be permanently satisfactory since the conflicts which occur in the life of action are likely to be found in the inner life as well. Moreover, the consciences of men differ widely. Conscience is the outcome of growth and education in so far as men are trained to approve some actions and to disapprove others. As men become increasingly free from rigid customs, and as it becomes evident that moral standards and practices depend to some extent on knowledge and cultural development, there is a tendency for men to direct their lives more and more on the basis of some set of values or a philosophy of life. Moral judgments may then be formulated on the basis of a reflective evaluation of principles and a careful examination of facts in relation to human life. Only when the latter stage is reached do we have reflective morality. The development of reflective morality does not mean the elimination of custom, law, or conscience; it means the addition of the reflective powers to those factors previously mentioned in the development of morality.

We have seen that the practices and values of morality grow out of life itself. They are the attempts of men to meet the needs of life under the specific conditions which they face. As intelligence and experience are enlarged, the requirements of personal and social welfare tend to be given more and more consideration. The story of the development of morality is a long story, which has been told in various books. This story may be traced in general terms, or it is possible to trace its development in particular areas of life, such as the family and the position of women, the administration of justice, and so forth.[1]

From the time of the early Greeks, when reflection upon the problems of conduct first took definite form, speculation on ethical problems has tended to fall into certain types of explanation. To live intelligently men must live consistently so far as it is possible. To live consistently, they need to guide their conduct by means of a unified standard of right or of good. So men have been asking and endeavoring to answer such questions as, "Why is one act right and another wrong?" "What is the greatest good which a man may seek?" The answers to such questions are the theories of morality or of ethics. The development of ethics represents man's efforts to discover the kind of life that is most worth living.

The Formalist or the Intuitionist will answer that the rightness of an act is an inherent quality of the act itself apart from circumstances. Immanuel Kant, 1724–1804, is an able representative of this position. Men should follow the line of duty revealed in the moral law which speaks within the man. The laws of nature are the laws of reason. When man's will is governed by reason, and not by inclination or desire, it is the moral law which legislates within the individual. If a man acts from a good motive or out of loyalty to a sense of duty, then the act is good regardless of the consequences or social effects. If a man performs an act from inclination or desire, the act has no intrinsic moral value. A detailed exposition of Kant's moral philosophy would require many pages. Every serious student of morality ought to be familiar with Kant. His influence has been powerful. Many of his statements like the following seem to express profound insight: "Act so as to use humanity, whether in your own person or in the person of another, always as an end, never as merely a means." Most men will rebel, however, against his attempt to separate moral principles from particular situations and to view the natural inclinations of men as something inferior. Why should an act lack moral worth because it is in line with our desires and inclinations? Shouldn't mature men find their happiness in following the path of duty? While we may need a certain amount of formalism in order to gain valid principles which are consistent, we need something more than formalism.

As distinct from formalism, the three classical theories of morality which we shall mention next, are teleological in their approach. That is, they judge conduct as right or wrong depending upon whether that conduct leads toward or away from some end or goal which is considered good. The Utilitarians, represented by John Stuart Mill, 1806–1873, stress happiness as the greatest good. Acts which lead toward happiness are good acts; those which lead toward pain are evil acts. This interpretation of the good life has had a long history. Among the ancient Greeks it was called Hedonism or Epicureanism. Sometimes it has taken egotistic and at other times altruistic forms. Since the time of Jeremy Bentham and John Stuart Mill in the nineteenth century, it has emphasized not the pleasure of the individual, but "the greatest happiness of the greatest number" of persons. While happiness is a good, there are many who feel that to accept pleasure or happiness as the standard of right and wrong is to place emphasis too exclusively upon feeling to the neglect of the intellectual, aesthetic, and religious side of man's nature. Happiness they think is a by-product and not an end-in-itself.

Herbert Spencer, 1820–1903, is a representative of those who stress "nature" or adaptation to environment as the goal of life. The natural laws of the evolutionary process lead in the direction of the good. This approach assumes that what is natural is right, that the standard of goodness is to be found in the processes at work in nature, or that the good is that which is achieved through natural selection. Does this approach confuse fitness in the biological sense with fitness in the moral sense? Does it disregard the fact that there are quite different levels of behavior? Are all results of the evolutionary process equally good? If it recognizes only "is" and not the sense of "ought," it is inadequate.

Writers from Plato, 427–347 B.C., to the present, have stressed the development of the person or the self as a thinking, feeling, and acting being, as the greatest good or the goal of life. This position is often called the Self-Realization theory. By Aristotle it was called Eudaemonism which is sometimes translated *well-being*. As a modern approach it stresses the harmonious development of all sides of man's nature and recognizes that personal welfare is bound up with social welfare. Evolution on the human level exhibits characteristics not found elsewhere in nature. Man's rational, ethical, and aesthetic nature is unique. Since men live in a growing world, even their goals tend to grow and to expand with new insight and new knowledge.

All the above views have had able supporters. In spite of major differences they agree in maintaining that there is an objective standard which is in some sense universal. Morality is not something purely relative and subjective. They agree that there is an obligation upon man to follow the good or to do the right if he can discover it. For any of these approaches the majority of issues will be decided in the same way. Each of the theories, if construed in a narrow sense is inadequate.

Each of the last three may be so explained that it includes the values stressed by the other views. In this case there are fewer objections to be offered.

These general theories of morality are formal and abstract and lack something when left by themselves. Ends separated from means and from particular life situations may be little more than sentimental indulgences which fail to stir men to action. I believe that of these general theories the theory of self-realization, if stated so that the social as well as the personal implications of personality are kept in mind, is the most satisfactory statement of the goal to be sought. Is Christian ethics a form and completion of the theory of self-realization?

A survey of the moral standards of peoples in all parts of the world will furnish further evidence that morals grow out of social needs and that these needs are fairly uniform among men. Whether it is the moral codes of the various Hindu groups, or of Confucius and Lao-tze in China, it is evident that life has certain great central demands and that these are met in very similar ways among the people of all races and groups. There are of course great differences in outlook and in individual regulations. Zoroastrianism conceives the universe as a battleground between light and darkness or between good and evil. In China there is a tendency to find the ultimate in the natural order of existence. The ethics of Islam approach nearer to a tribal morality and have less of the universal elements. In the East there is a tendency toward resignation and quietness, whereas in Western civilization there is greater emphasis on the positive fulfillment of life. Yet in spite of these differences, one finds much the same things approved and the same things condemned. We find the same general principles underlying the moral codes of these groups. For example, such acts as killing, stealing, lying, deceit, and the like are forbidden. There are among all people definite regulations, both positive and negative, regarding sex relations. Such virtues as justice, courage, loyalty to the group, benevolence or helpfulness to the weak and suffering, obedience to elders, parents, or those in authority, and filial piety, are practically universally commended.

Various circumstances and outlooks, such as social and political organization and world view, tend to affect the moral ideal. In peaceful patriarchal societies, benevolence and filial piety may take precedence; in a feudal society, courage and honor may be emphasized; while countries with absolute rulers may stress obedience and respect for those in control. With the rise of democracies, justice may become broader in its scope so that men come to think in terms of a common good for all men. A moral code is the accepted and approved way of acting within the bounds of a human group. It is a way established by experience, often with the aid of reflection, in the interests of living.

Christian Ethics — Two Types

I

Taking, for the time, Christian ethics as the ethical outlook found among groups of Christians, we find that it may express itself in one of two general patterns. First, there are those Christians who claim that Christianity is a deposit of final and absolute truth and a definite program which has been completely revealed by God to men. The duty of individual Christians is, therefore, to discover the content of this revelation and to obey it. This view has had many supporters throughout the history of the church. It represents the point of view of the "orthodox" of the earlier centuries and of the fundamentalists in recent decades. Many who hold this position are unaware of, or reject, the results of recent historical and biblical studies. According to this first approach, Christianity is an authoritative system and the chief virtue is obedience. Morality is kept strictly theological, and ethical duties stand out by themselves with no reason or justification except that they are believed to be the will of God. God, the Bible, or the Church lays down rules of action which are to be obeyed. God does not require certain things because they are right; they are right because God does require them.

More recently this authoritarian view has been set forth in a different form by exponents of the "crisis theology," who at least nominally accept the results of historical and biblical criticism. Karl Barth, Emil Brunner, and others have been leaders in this movement. In his book, *The Divine Imperative,* Emil Brunner tells us that "the good is simply and solely the will of God," and that "the good is based solely on God's transcendent revelation." [2] What God does and wills is right and good. All that opposes the will of God is wrong and evil. Good is always the gift of God and God is wholly transcendent. The good is only achieved when it is performed "solely in the spirit of love of God and in obedience to His command." This is the imperative of faith. Good is always the gift of God, and consists in doing what He wills at any particular moment. God's word is found in the Scripture as interpreted through the aid of the Spirit. Such an approach makes Christian ethics supra-historical and supernatural in the extreme. No revelation of God is found in nature or in history.

According to the above view there is a wide gap between Christian ethics and philosophical ethics. They move in different realms entirely. Philosophical ethics arises from a study of human nature, conduct, and history, and by a process of reasoning which formulates ideals and standards. The difference, however, is not so much a question of accepting the Will of God as the way in which we believe that God's will is discovered or disclosed.

II

In the second place, Christian ethics, for an increasingly large number of Christians, expresses itself in dynamic and functional terms. Men are encouraged to discover empirically the tasks that need to be done; then these tasks are seen as a part of man's duty to God. Loyalty to Christ means loyalty to the best possible life in the situation in which men find themselves. Goals or ends of life, rather than rules of action, are disclosed to men. The spirit of Jesus is expressed as a supreme concern for human values. The Christian life is thus a quest for the good under the inspiration of devotion to the ideals of Jesus.

What is Christian morality or Christian ethics and where can we find an accurate statement of it? Is it the teaching of the Christian Bible? Whose interpretation of the Bible? Is it the teachings of the Christian Church? Which Church and when? Many persons would answer that Christian morality is that which is found in the teachings of Jesus as found in the Gospels, or they would say that it is the ethical principles held by the Christian Church through the centuries. Let us examine such answers.

The Ethics of Jesus

In our attempt to discover the ethics of Jesus certain difficulties present themselves. Jesus himself left no writings. The Gospel records which are our main sources of his teachings and his life are quite obviously not shorthand reports of conversation and of events. They are interpretations written down at a later time, and they do not always agree as to what was said or what happened. The original eyewitnesses and early narrators not only had to make a selection of materials, but their accounts were based on their assumptions and sense of values. The numerous lives of Jesus, written down through the ages, make clear the effect of the current psychology and philosophy upon the interpretations and selection of materials.

The teachings of Jesus, moreover, were apparently adapted to the particular problems which he was facing. He left no systematic moral code as a complete guide for his followers. Some of the problems which existed in his day, we do not have, at least in the same form. Some problems which we face did not exist at that time. What should be our attitude toward a League of Nations, "Union Now," labor unions, labor espionage, industrial sabotage, holding companies, birth control, and many other problems which are distinctly modern? The social, economic, and political conditions, as well as scientific views and cosmologies, have changed. He lived and talked in a simple pastoral and agricultural civilization, whereas today most men live in a highly complex industrial society. A large part of his teachings were in the form of illustrative stories or parables which arose out of specific conditions. Since this is the case, people have been able to take his sayings and use them to support quite different and often opposite positions, to support pacifism as well as the use of force, to support a purely individualistic as well as a social gospel.

Jesus did not formulate an entirely new set of ethical principles. In fact it has been said that practically every element of his teachings had been brought out by some prophet or teacher who preceded him. The Hebrew prophets, the philosophers of Greece, Confucius, and the moral leaders of many ancient civilizations had brought forth many of the truths that Jesus taught. Rather than detracting from the work of Jesus, they merely tend to add to their trustworthiness and to confirm the view that God works in the social process and that moral and religious truths are social products. Jesus brought together the central truths of religion and morality in a simple, direct way and embodied them in his own life as no other person has done. Christianity inherited an especially rich legacy of morality from the Jews. Jesus, in acknowledging this, said: "Think not that I came to destroy the law or the prophets. I came not to destroy but to fulfill." He took the rich contribution of his people and gave it new form. Parts of it he brushed aside; other parts he changed and expanded; still other parts he interpreted and re-emphasized. His originality is seen in the fact that he could ignore the older authorities and speak with such freshness and conviction that men said that he spoke with authority. He took the rather exclusive and nationalistic morality of the Jews of his day and made it into a universalism that embraced all men. He placed the duties and responsibilities of men in relation to their fellowmen and to God in a truer perspective. Upon the movement which he started, he left the indelible stamp of personal sincerity and goodness, vicarious sacrifice, and companionship with God. Christians believe that he revealed the nature of God and the heart of the moral problem as did no one else before or since his time.

Who is the real Jesus, and how should he be interpreted? If this question could be answered finally and definitely it would assist us in discovering the content and purpose of his ethical teaching. Throughout history, and at the present time, there are widely varying interpretations of Jesus, set forth by able scholars and religious leaders. Shall we follow such interpretations as Johannes Weiss, Albert Schweitzer, and Alfred Loisy, and make him a consistent eschatologist who looked for the immediate supernatural coming of the reign of God and

for his own return as the glorified Messiah? If we emphasize
the apocalyptic elements in his teachings, it may be true that
his ethics were purely an "interim ethics," as some claim. If
this is the true interpretation, what is the application of these
teachings for today? On the other hand, shall we follow the
Kantian-Ritschlian interpretation of the Kingdom of God
within the heart and set forth a religion that is spiritual and
ethical in its emphasis? Or was Jesus a social reformer seeking social justice and social reform? For a discussion of the
details of these and related questions, I refer the reader to
books like McCown, *The Search for the Real Jesus.*

Christian Ethics Historically Conditioned

Has the church throughout the centuries held to one set of
principles or to one interpretation of Christian ethics and conduct? A careful study of the history of the Christian belief
and practice will indicate that the teachings of Jesus as well
as Christian duties and rights were interpreted in terms of the
assumptions and the social outlook of the age. In different
periods Christians have stressed different virtues. Besides faith,
hope, and love, the early Christians emphasized loyalty and
obedience to the church, martyrdom or willingness to suffer,
patient endurance, almsgiving, conquest over the flesh, stew-
ardship, and the like. While the Christians were a persecuted
minority group, there was an effort to keep the church and
individuals true to Christ, not to change the world. The early
Christians were concerned with practical problems of conduct,
while the later Christians became engrossed in cosmological
and speculative issues as well as in problems of church organization and the nature of the sacraments. The early Christians
thought of themselves as sojourners or pilgrims on the earth
and they were especially concerned to keep themselves pure.

Since they looked for escape from the world rather than for means of changing it, they felt that such organizations of society as slavery were of no fundamental consequence and would soon pass away.

The Epistles of Paul are concerned with ethical issues, such as the virtues, the vices, sin, righteousness, and the law, as well as with theological ideas—God, redemption, and immortality. While Paul felt that he was continuing the work of Jesus, he seldom pointed to the example of Jesus and rarely mentioned his earthly career. The Christian life is a continuation and completion of the moral development seen in Hebrew history. Even the Gentiles have a "law written in their hearts" and "do by nature the things contained in the law." [3] Thus the witness of God is found among all men. Paul's universal emphasis is seen in his claim that Christ died for all men. His social emphasis is seen in his statements that we are members one of another, and that we must bear one another's burdens.

The first century Christians were likely to stress escape from the world rather than steps to change it. As time went on, however, and especially after Christianity became an accepted and an official religion, this outlook began to change. During the first century there was a tendency to stress the simple, homely virtues which would be included in the love of God, love for one's fellowmen, purity and sincerity of purpose and conduct. This will be seen in the writings of Clement of Rome, Polycarp, also in the *Epistle of Barnabas,* the *Didache* or *Teaching of the Twelve Apostles,* and the *Shepard of Hermas.* Ignatius, Bishop of Antioch, late in the first century, stressed the importance of right beliefs for moral conduct. Faith is the beginning and love the end of the Christian life. Jesus provides an object of imitation which the Christian must strive to follow.

Justin Martyr, writing in the second century, was one of a

group of early Christians, including Irenaeus, Clement of Alexandria, and Origen, who made much of the *logos* doctrine and who tended to restate the Christian message in terms of Greek thought. According to Justin Martyr, Christianity is the goal and complete expression of Greek ethical principles since it is a morality of universal reason (*logos*). The Christian life is based in Christ, the eternal *logos,* and there are moral qualifications for entrance into this fellowship. In his *Apology* before the emperor he attempted to show that the Christians were both a God-fearing and a virtuous group and that the charges against them were false.

Origen, 182–251 A.D., was one of the outstanding Christian leaders of the early third century. While his main contributions are theological rather than ethical, he did give some attention to morals. Man is made in the image of God and the Christian life is a struggle to attain as nearly as possible to perfection. For the good man, life is a struggle on the side of Christ against Satan and his hosts. There is, according to Origen, a natural law written in the hearts of men so that there is a similarity of moral ideas and convictions among men. This law has been proclaimed by the prophets and leaders of old and by Jesus. Philosophical and Christian moral ideas are not basically opposed to each other. Christian morality, however, is personal and positive and emphasizes devotion to God as the goal. The Christian, moreover, acknowledges his debt of gratitude and love toward God and joins in fellowship with other men to worship Him. The tendency of this period toward asceticism is also seen in the writings of Origen. The spiritual and the sensuous stand in sharp opposition. Humility is one of the main virtues and he commends fasting, almsgiving, and virginity. Pride, arrogance, and vanity are among the greatest of vices. The petition for daily bread, in the Lord's Prayer, is not for physical but for spiritual nourish-

ment, he thinks. Penitence is the cure for the stained soul in
its search for perfection.

Whereas the Greek or Eastern Church Fathers represented
Christianity as more continuous with, though an advance over,
ancient Greek thought, the Latin or Western (Roman)
Fathers tended more to the view that Christianity is morally
something new or different, involving a break with the past,
and implying a rejection of Gentile ideas and conduct. Since
religious and ethical thinking in the West was so thoroughly
dominated by Augustine from the fifth century to the era of
the Reformation, we shall turn to him next.

Augustine, 354–430 A.D., systematized the ethics of the early
church and brought it more completely within the sacramental
and ecclesiastical system. His reaction against the pagan life
of his times, in which he had participated so freely as a youth,
was sudden and complete. In his *Confessions* he tells about
his great emotional experience during his conversion. This
experience affected his doctrine of sin and grace. Salvation
meant a complete break with the past and he felt he could
choose the good as he was unable to do before. He came to
believe that the church was the institution through which God
supplies the transforming grace that makes men good. The
means are the sacraments of the church. Men may have a
supernaturally created moral life through the sacraments. In
this way Augustine brought the sacraments to a position of
primacy in the ethical life.

In his great work, *The City of God,* Augustine distinguished
between "the City of God" which is predestined to exist
eternally and "the earthly city" which will pass away. In the
one city men live according to the spirit; in the other, they live
according to the flesh. At present the two cities exist side by
side. The city of God is partly in heaven and partly on earth.
The Kingdom of God includes the church and the community

of morally creative people. From this it follows that we find two kinds of Christianity, one represented by the clergy and the monastic orders and the other by those who are outside these orders. The church provides the means by which those who compromise to a greater extent with the world may attain a Christian life. There may be religious vocations here in the present social order. The Christian must use his vocation, whatever it is, to the glory of God. Since vocations in this way may become Christian, we may hope for a Christianizing of the social order. After Augustine, Christian ethics begins to have a wider significance. Whereas in primitive Christianity, many felt that the Christian life must be that of a separatist, now the separateness of the Christian consists in the supernatural endowment through grace or the sacraments of the church.

Among the philosophers, Plato is the one who comes closest to Christianity in the opinion of Augustine. Plato taught that God is the true and highest good. Man is to seek union with God and strive for likeness with Him. True love of God will reveal itself in respect for one's self and regard for one's neighbor. Augustine brought together in one system, which had its basis in God, the virtues of the Greeks and the central Christian attitude of faith, hope, and love. Whereas the Greeks placed emphasis on knowledge and wisdom, Augustine tended to stress the elements of will and commitment to God or to the church.

During the medieval period, as the result of the growth of asceticism, humility, self-abnegation, and self-mortification tended to be prominent virtues. In some of the religious orders, poverty, chastity, and obedience were the supreme virtues. Thomas Aquinas, 1225 or 1227–1274, one of the great minds of the middle ages, was especially influenced by Augustine and Aristotle. He was the great systematizer of Scholasticism. He brought together into one system the ecclesiastical and the cultural ideals of his day and attempted to make clear that man is living in relation to a natural and to a supernatural world. Through reason, man may know the moral virtues of prudence, justice, temperance, and fortitude, and the intellectual virtues of understanding, knowledge, and wisdom. Only by revelation may man know the theological virtues of faith, hope, and love.

Man, created with wisdom and goodness, was lost by the Fall and has now no claim on eternal life. The first essential to a good life is a gift of grace to overcome the ravages of the Fall. Not only has this gift of grace been provided, but the principles of ethics are given in a divinely ordained system of laws. The Christian man conforms to the law of God by the correct use of his reason and by accepting the revealed doctrines. Obedience and reverence for authority are supreme virtues. While all are to be equal in eternal life there is a divine organization of society which provides for different functions and different duties. This is the basis for the various classes and orders in society. There are no universal duties applicable to all men. Each man has his station in life and there are special privileges and duties of rulers and subjects, priests and laymen. The family, the state, industrial life, and the clergy are all ordained by God for the carrying out of special functions. The outcome of such an approach tends to be the reinforcement of law and order at every point.

Modern Roman Catholicism follows Thomas Aquinas fairly closely. It has been compelled, however, to adjust itself, to some extent, to modern conditions and movements like the rise of Protestantism or the divisions within Christianity, the rise of secular governments and democratic institutions, and the development of modern science.

The Protestant Reformation was part of a general movement of life which finally broke many of the bonds of medieval society and changed Western civilization. The Protestants stressed the immediate, direct, or personal relationship and loyalty to a personal God. Justification was by faith alone. There was the universal priesthood of believers and consequently the system of mediation set up by the medieval church with its many sacraments, priestly groups, saints, intercessions, fasts and feasts, and legalistic regulations, tended to drop away. It was a marked simplification of belief and practice. The Protestants also placed emphasis upon the worth of the natural, human relationships. God could be found in the common places. Family life was sacred and not a concession to the flesh. Asceticism and monasticism were abandoned. God was in nature, in history, and in man. Salvation was inner, personal, and ethical.

The above principles and points of emphasis in the Protestant Reformation were only vaguely understood. At first many of the leaders thought that it was just a reform movement within the older church. Before long there was a new legalism and authoritarianism to take the place of the older system. Consequently the reformation has been going on, or should we say, "breaking out anew," from time to time.

Martin Luther protested against many practices in the church of his day, especially the sale of indulgences which he considered immoral. He stressed the inner religious life or the experience of salvation. "The just shall live by faith alone." Good works are of no avail. Every person is by nature depraved. Morality begins in the regeneration of the person. Luther's ethics was fundamentally personal. God looks on the persons who act, not upon the deeds done. There is little tendency to question the state or the institutions of society. The Christian accepts the world as he finds it and expresses Christian love to others.

John Calvin set forth a more legalistic interpretation which stressed the Bible and especially the Decalogue as the law of God and the rule of life. It is the declaration of natural law and of that conscience which has been engraved by God on the minds of men. He directed much of his time and energy to the suppression of the immorality of the society of his day. Governments, he felt, exist to enforce the will of God and to restrain evildoers. They must be organized in conformity to God's will and accept the Bible as the constitution. The leaders of the church know what the Bible teaches and therefore are able to assist the rulers. Christian ethics are thus defined in terms of an aggressive, ecclesiastical regulation of evils in society. In this way the Calvinists believe in Christianizing the social order. Calvin felt that devotion to one's "calling" was a religious duty. To work is to worship, and worldly success is an indication of the blessing of God. He stressed the virtues of reverence, chastity, sobriety, frugality, industry, and honesty.

With the growth of Protestantism there was a definite tendency to emphasize the virtues related to the natural relations and associations of men and to reject the dual standard which tended to separate the laity and the clerical orders. The rise of Puritanism and of the Middle Class interested in commerce and industry led to an austere code of morality which emphasized the authority of the Scriptures and frowned on the spontaneous enjoyment of life in this world. Every man had a calling, and unwillingness to work or lack of worldly success was an indication of lack of grace. Industry, initiative, thrift, and benevolence came to be stressed as the virtues of a *laissez-faire* economy.

Since the time of the Reformation many statements of Christian ethics have been set forth so that it is difficult to take any one formulation and insist that that is the true Christian ethics. There have been those, like the Brethren and other fundamentalist groups that have clung to a simple and literal adherence to the letter of Scripture in the belief that God dictated a book and put it into the hands of his children to guide thinking and practice. The adherents of the Crisis theology have set forth an "Apocalyptic Ethics." Good is always the gift of a God who is wholly transcendent or above and beyond the world, and who comes to us in a crisis. The basis of genuine morality is supernatural and supra-historical although it may be the revelation of the Word of God. Many persons, like Tolstoy, have emphasized or perhaps exaggerated some one element in the teachings of Jesus or in Christian history. Tolstoy felt that the injunction "Love thine enemies" was the fundamental principle of Christian ethics and that consequently man must not resist evil by violence. He extended the idea of renunciation to include the elimination of all political authority and the use of courts of law.

There has been a large and increasing group of Christians who have emphasized the "naturalness" of Christian morality. Bishop Joseph Butler, writing in the eighteenth century, maintained that Christianity is the "republication" of natural religion and that Christian ethics is in conformity with the nature of mankind. He recognized two sources of ethical knowledge: nature and reason on the one hand, and revelation through the Bible on the other. God is the one source of the moral law in conscience, in the constitution of nature, and in the Scriptures. In *Christian Morality,* the Gifford Lectures for 1935–1936, H. H. Henson gives as his assumption "that the morality which Christ's religion properly requires is precisely that which the conscience and reason of modernly civilized men approve." [4] Human nature, far from being static, is a developing and an integral part of a developing universe. That which is natural at one stage of this development may be archaic and even apparently false at a later stage. All religion is natural, and all religion is revealed since religion pre-supposes a religious capacity in men. In a similar way Christian morality is the highest version of natural morality.

Today we find Formalists, Utilitarians, and supporters of the theory of Self-Realization, each ready to claim that the ethics of Jesus falls within that particular ethical outlook. We have seen that many Christians have felt that ethics in general and Christian ethics are not basically opposed, but grow out of the same roots and problems of human living.

There is a growing tendency for Christians to interpret morality as empirical and functional. The fact, however, that it is dynamic does not detract from its Christian nature since Christianity is a growing living religion in a growing world. Today there is a call for renewed emphasis upon such virtues as tolerance and co-operativeness as well as for many of the older virtues like courage and justice. Whereas the medieval period may have denied the worth of certain values associated with the physical body and with economic goods, it is possible that our own age overstresses those values to the neglect of the non-material values.

The Nature of Christian Morality

Christian morality, as we know it in modern society, is the result of a long period of development in the course of which new elements from various sources have been assimilated. All genuine human values are and should be incorporated in the Christian ideal. While some Christians have undoubtedly thought it to be static, and while the thinking of these individuals may have remained static throughout life, Christian ethics has never been a closed or static thing. It is not to be completely identified with the ethics of the Greeks, nor of the Hebrews, nor of the New Testament, nor of any previous period in the history of Christianity. No one leader has made a complete and final formulation of it, and we cannot expect to do so today. We can merely say that some forms and statements of it are more mature than others. Christian morality has taken into itself the gains and the insights of continuous experiments in Christian living. It brings us elements that are rooted in the best traditions of the past as well as absorbing into itself new insights from its growing experiences and insights.

Christian morality, while maintaining its connection with its founder and with the past, while acknowledging its great debt to them, and while embodying certain persistent and fundamental attitudes, is still in the making. It continually absorbs new elements, since it takes into itself whatever is intellectually acceptable and morally sound in the society in which it expresses itself. This dynamic nature is one evidence of its power and permanence—we may even say, of its finality. A movement that ceases to grow and to become more mature soon ceases to be good.

The above statements do not mean that any morality that is growing is Christian. In fact, there are many codes of living in the modern world that are definitely anti-Christian and, from our point of view, immoral. They do indicate that both general ethics and Christian ethics have grown and developed and that there has been an interaction between the different movements. Thinkers, claiming loyalty to Christian ideals, have contributed to the development of philosophical and general ethics. Various representatives of the classical schools of ethics have claimed that they represented the Christian approach. Each of the more significant movements in the field of ethics have been modified and enriched by the insights and criticisms offered by the representatives of other approaches.

From the brief survey of the history of morality and of

Christian ethics which we have made in this chapter it is evident that Christian ethics is not something entirely separate and distinct, nor can we say that it means simply the teachings of Jesus, the ethical ideals of the New Testament, or the teachings of any section of the Christian Church. There are, however, certain common elements or assumptions, certain basic attitudes which any ethics that can rightly be called "Christian" will include.

Let us consider these traits briefly before concluding the chapter. In the first place, in Christian ethics the "good" has been personalized and stated in terms of devotion or loyalty to Jesus. He so impressed his spirit and way of life upon an historical movement that it will continue to be stated in terms of his dynamic and unique personality. Loyalty to Jesus thus means loyalty to the best possible life in the situation in which men discover themselves. Christian ethics thus remains loyal to Jesus while it is able, at the same time, to associate itself with the forward movement of mankind.

In the second place, Christian ethics specializes in getting men to want the better life. To the motives of general ethics, Christianity adds the attraction of a great moral personality. Such ethics becomes one of attraction and aspiration, and not one driven mainly by a sense of duty or by the pressure of society or of the environment. One problem before men is to discover the actual direction in which the good lies. A still greater problem frequently is to act or to get persons to act in that direction. "The spirit is willing but the flesh is weak." To the motives of general ethics, Christianity adds the more personal element of fellowship in a religious community. Christian ethics also views personal moral growth and social welfare as part of one's religious endeavor.

In the third place, Christian ethics is based on a distinctively Christian interpretation of the nature of man and of the universe. If the Christian interpretation of life is different from the non-Christian, then an ethics based on that interpretation will differ in point of view and in spirit. Christian ethics is based on a theistic world view which separates it from all non-theistic systems. Insofar as Christianity differs from other religious world views, like the Buddhistic and Mohammedan, in its interpretations and spirit, its ethics will likewise differ. Among the implications of this world view are a conception of the worth of persons as persons, and a view of the universe as purposeful. Christian ethics sees human nature as charged with great possibilities for growth or improvement. It relates the quest for the good life to the larger cosmic whole in which humanity is operating. Wrongdoing is not only immoral, it is sin against God.

In the fourth place, Christian ethics differs considerably in spirit and emphasis from the classical systems and from modern philosophical systems of ethics. Greek conceptions of ethics have been more self-centered or concerned with a man's treatment of himself. They have stressed wisdom, courage, self-control, justice, and the like. "Moderation in all things" is a phrase which is characteristically Greek. Philosophical ethics, on the whole, has tended to be formal and "intellectualistic" in its outlook and attitude. Christian ethics, on the other hand, has stressed love for one's neighbor and the clean heart or the inward side of moral experience. Christian ethics is an ethics of the spirit, inner and free, which emphasizes creative good will and redemptive love.

CHAPTER IV

MARKS OF A MATURE MORALITY

MORALITY IS NOT A SET of rigid rules or a fixed body
of "truth" applicable to all times and to every condition. Morality is dynamic and growing. We live
in a world in which circumstances differ from time to time
and place to place. Ethical goals and principles, to be of
value and applicable to all persons, must be fairly general so
that they may be applied to different circumstances. On the
other hand, they must be sufficiently specific so that they will
not be lost in vagueness. If they are too formal and abstract,
they will not give sufficient guidance in the concrete problems
of life. The problem facing men is not only how to live in a
world like this, but how to live *well*. The following marks of
a mature morality are set forth as suggestions. There is some
overlapping and some of them might be taken as implications of others. They are stated as they are because each statement places an emphasis upon something which seems to need
emphasis. In the opinion of the author, the nearer we approach these ideals the more nearly mature we shall be, and
the higher our morality.

I. *A Mature Morality judges an act right or wrong on
the basis of its effect upon persons or upon human
welfare.*

To the person who is morally mature an act that is beneficial to persons or to humanity is a good act. An act that is
harmful or detrimental is a bad act, regardless of whether

the community approves or disapproves. The purpose of a study of moral standards is to lead men more consciously to consider what is most worthwhile in life, to approve conduct and character which has beneficial results, and to condemn conduct which is harmful. The *right* is based on the *good*, the good is that which has *value for persons*.

Now why do we designate persons as the basis of values? In the first place, because only in persons, in men and in women, do we find certain qualities and characteristics that seem of supreme worth. Only persons are centers of feeling and can experience joys and sorrows, pleasures and pains. Only in persons do we find self-consciousness, including memory and imagination. Only in persons do we find the power of deliberation or reflective thinking and the ability to distinguish between right and wrong.

Since there are many false notions of persons, we shall need to make our meaning as clear as possible. Man is in part a physico-chemical system, and some things in connection with him can be described in terms of mechanism. Man is in part an animal organism or a physiological system. He has the characteristics of protoplasm including metabolism and sensitivity. He grows and reproduces as do other animals. But these mechanical and these animal processes are not the distinctive things about man. While they affect his entire being, they are not distinctive of man as a person. He has additional powers and characteristics which place him on a level by himself. There is the experience of *self-identity* or unity that runs through all man's separate experiences. Man is not only a sensitive and conscious being, but he is *self-conscious*. He is a *self* not only with a present, but with a past and a future, with *memory* and *imagination*. Man also has the power of *reflective thinking or reason,* which is a distinctive human trait. While animals can form precepts, apparently man alone can form concepts. The power of deliberation, of distinguishing between truth and falsity, or of discriminating between issues and weighing and comparing them, is the basis of human progress. Man has the *power of ethical discrimination.* From the point of view of ethics, a person is one who is conscious of distinctions between right and wrong; one who is *responsible for his acts* and who is capable of feeling a sense of innocence or of guilt. A person in this sense has *a degree of freedom* or of *the power of choice.* From the point of view of the law, a person is one who has both rights and duties. The concept "person" implies that there are present both *meanings* and *values.* These meanings and values are the basis for science, philosophy, art, religion, and for human fellowship. We are using, then, the terms "person" and "personality" for the sum of these qualities which are distinctive of human beings. The terms are creative and dynamic, not static or fixed.

In the second place, we designate persons as the basis of values, because this is an ethical judgment, perhaps intuitive, which is at the heart of many religious and ethical systems. As well as in Christianity, it is found in Greek Stoicism and in Buddhism. It is implied or stated in the moral philosophies of Plato, Aristotle, Kant, Hegel, T. H. Green, the Utilitarians, and the Humanists. "Live so that you increase life" has been the advice of men from Socrates and Jesus in ancient times to philosophers like G. E. Moore and John Dewey among our contemporaries. We have previously pointed out that if one consents to live, he is to some extent valuing life.

Human intelligence and the central emphasis in Christian teaching appear to be one in emphasizing life, or persons, or human welfare as the locus of value, and the basis of the distinction between right and wrong. The development of per-

sons or selves is right and the neglect or abuse of life's endowment is wrong. On one occasion men came to Jesus asking
him whether it was right to pluck corn and eat it on the
Sabbath Day. Jesus could have referred to many rules bear-
ing upon the use of the Sabbath. Instead he merely said: "The
Sabbath was made for man, not man for the Sabbath." His
attitude is best expressed as a supreme concern for human
values. Whatever promoted human life and welfare merited
his approval. Whatever was detrimental to human life or
degrading, he vigorously condemned.

On the individual side, man has both rights and duties. He
has the duty to develop his own potentialities, physically, intellectually, morally, and spiritually. He has a right to the means
which are necessary to live a truly human, that is, a well-
rounded, personal life. He needs to become a free, creative
personality. There is an interesting story that Fichte, the
German philosopher and exponent of idealism, gave a party
when his small boy was first able to pronounce the word "I."
It represented the dawning of selfhood and meant that from
then on the lad was really a person.

On the social side, if persons are of supreme worth, then
every man ought to have the means necessary to develop his
powers and his capabilities. He ought to be able to live a full
life or to realize and express his personality. The valid test,
then, of any act, any system or institution, or any social program, will be its effect upon persons, selves, or the scope which
it gives for the development of human personality. Action is
right if it leads to my personal development and to a more
harmonious personal and social life. Action is wrong if it is
detrimental to the individual or to society. We need some
term which would express personal development in the direction of goodness, truth, and beauty, and which would also

include social welfare, or even the greatest happiness of the greatest number.

Let us turn, briefly, to the application of this principle in social relations. Is modern society organized around the principle of the supreme worth of human personality? Quite obviously this is not the case today. The fundamental issue of our age is whether our lives and society are to be based on a recognition of the principle of personality and of fellowship, or whether they are to be organized around the principle of possession, of domination, or of power. This conflict between these two ideals can be seen in all phases of life, individual and social.

Today the way of power is in the ascendancy, and the world is organized too largely on the basis of domination and control. Men and groups tend to order their lives and activities with a view to domination. Hosts of men seek to meet their fellows as superiors, and to use them for their own purposes. Men, like machines, are manipulated and controlled for the benefit of the manipulator. In the realm of politics the way of power may express itself as machine politics where the attempt is made to manipulate the electorate and to maintain control. In its more extreme form it expresses itself as dictatorship or totalitarianism. In the realm of trade, business, or of economics, the way of power is the way of the "acquisitive society," which insists upon the right to pursue self-interest primarily. Gain may be divorced from service and become an end in itself. Social benefit is secondary or incidental. Men are judged and respected for their possessions of wealth and property. Such an attitude may lead to the elevation of a social class which claims special privileges, but which repudiates any responsibility for the conditions of society.

The way of personality and of fellowship has been advo-

cated by a great many men, past and present. On this basis
a man seeks to meet his fellowmen as friends and equals in a
common task, realizing that the great values of life can never
be the exclusive right or possession of any person. In this way
self-surrender and self-expansion go hand in hand, since man
learns to find his joy and satisfaction in ways and in things
that bring happiness to others. This way of life also finds some
expression in trade and politics as well as in more intimate
personal relations. In the realm of economics the way of fellowship is taking the form of a demand for a greater degree
of co-operation and for a functional society, a society in which
trade and commerce are subordinated to the social purposes
for which they are carried on. Men should be respected for
their acts of creation, for service rendered, for responsibility,
and for their qualities of personality. Part of the appeal of
the co-operative movement has been the fact that, through
it, a method has been found which cultivates fellowship as
well as economic well-being. In the way of fellowship, the
men in authority use power *for* others rather than *over*
others.

If persons are of supreme worth, then other persons are as
valuable as I am or as you are. The things which human
beings possess in common are of more importance than those
things which divide them. Men everywhere possess much the
same capacities variously blended. They have the same appetites, strivings, interests, and needs. They crave companionship and fellowship. They hope and fear, love and hate, suffer
and rejoice. The man who can deny that other human beings
have rights and needs comparable to his own is hard and
inhuman. Only in and through other lives does any one life
come to fulfillment. Men find life by sharing it and by increasing life everywhere. This brings us directly to our next point.

II. *A Mature Morality is one in which concern for persons expresses itself in a spirit of love or selflessness,
and even when necessary in self-sacrifice. This spirit
of love at its highest embraces the entire human
family.*

The choice of a single word for the quality of character
we wish to express is difficult. *Love* is one of the best terms and
it has been widely used by Christians. Yet it means quite different things to different persons. We shall use it in the sense
of the sympathetic understanding, desire for, and earnest
effort to promote the good of others. *Selflessness* and *unselfishness* carry much the same meaning. *Altruism* is an ethical term,
the opposite of egoism, which embraces the moral motives
which induce a man to promote the good of others. *Self-denial*
is rather negative in its implications. *Self-sacrifice,* the act of
sacrificing oneself for others, probably ought to be reserved
for the more heroic occasions of life.

In our chapter on The Basis of a Moral Order, we pointed
out that the basis of the ideal of love or unselfishness is the
psychological fact of human sympathy. Man has been made
to live, and laugh, and love with other human beings, and
he cannot have peace and satisfaction within his own life
unless he does so. Consequently, it is not surprising to find
that the great moral teachers and leaders of the race have
stressed unselfishness as the very essence of morality. The Christian "Golden Rule," "Do unto others as ye would that men
should do unto you," also stated negatively by Confucius,
might be termed the supreme law of morals.

In Christianity the emphasis on love grows out of the Christian philosophy of life. Central in Christianity is the faith that
the final power in the universe is Spirit, not matter nor blind

force, and that love is the highest expression of Spirit. The cross has been the symbol of sacrificial love and bears the most moving testimony to its reality and power in the world. Consequently, love for one's fellowmen and for God has been stressed as the supreme virtue. Love is more than justice, it is "the transference of interest from the I to the Thou." It does not stop at mere rights and duties; it is concerned with the other person for his own sake. It has been called "the whole law" and "the fulfillment of the law."

The self-regarding and the other-regarding dispositions of man are subtly blended in his make-up. Neither can gain adequate satisfaction without the other. While our altruistic impulses are nearly as deep-rooted in human nature as our self-regarding impulses, there has been a tendency for them to be developed more slowly and to be expressed first in small groups. The child is born into the family circle. For a time he is a little individualist and recognizes no rights but his own bodily needs. In a short time, however, he becomes a member of the family group sharing their joys and burdens. He soon begins to widen his mental horizons, interests, and sympathies to take in the neighborhood or the community with its various institutions. At least politically, he eventually comes to think in terms of the state or the nation. Even though it frequently does stop, his development ought not to stop short of interests and sympathies that are world wide. In the growth of society, somewhat the same steps can be seen. Man first expressed the law of altruism in the close and continuous contacts of the family group. Beyond the family, the tribal stage came next and was followed in turn by the growth of nationalism as the area of group consciousness widened. Only gradually and among comparatively small groups has man come to realize that the same principle of altruism applies universally to all human beings. Christianity has been attempting to

organize human life on the basis of the family pattern and
ideal since it is there that a person counts, not for what he
has, but for what he is. In the family we tend to see human
life at its best. Our international affairs wait not only for
peace and new organization, but for the imaginative inter-
weaving of the life of all peoples in this design of friendly
co-operative living.

In their expressions of sympathy and love, men are limited by the range of their imagination and insight, the breadth
of their experience and awareness, and the energy which they
have available. The cry of the injured child in our presence
will arouse us as a report of an injury in the next county will
not. If we have lost loved ones we can understand more adequately the sorrows of bereavement. When our energies and
resources are limited we choose to help those near us in blood
and in space. In a very real sense "morality begins at home."
If it is not expressed in the intimate relations, it is not likely
to find expression elsewhere. While it is difficult, if not impossible, to love "humanity" with the same zeal and warmth with
which one is attached to intimate friends, one's ideal ought
not to be less. While our failure to measure up to the ideal
may be colossal, the life of love, of unselfishness, and of mutual
aid is central in our conception of the noble life, and at the
basis of the institutions, the customs, and the laws, underlying
our democratic way of life. A willingness to sacrifice not only
for our own future good, but for the good of the community
and of the world, seems essential for the fullest realization of
our selfhood and for the advancement of our civilization.

Our failure as a people to live the life of selflessness should
not lead us to overlook those shining examples of devotion to the
common good which lead some men to make even the supreme
sacrifice for a cause in which they believe. Some men in all
ages have joyfully chosen the way of the cross. Men are choos-

ing it today as the following letter, written by a young aviator
of the Royal Air Force to his mother, will indicate: "Those
who serve England must expect nothing from her; we debase
ourselves if we regard our country as merely a place in which
to eat and sleep. . . . We are faced with the greatest organized challenge to Christianity and civilization that the world
has ever seen, and I count myself lucky and honored to be
the right age and fully trained to throw my full weight into
the scale. For this I have to thank you. . . . I have no fear
of death, only a queer elation. . . ." [1] The young aviator
made the supreme sacrifice.

In speaking of the range of active sympathy, W. P. Montague says, "To feel the values of other beings as your values
is to enrich and enlarge your own being and to make your life
vicariously, but quite genuinely, more abundant. Man's distinctive glory lies not in the extent of his knowledge, but in
the extent of his sympathy and in the vast co-operative life
which is thereby made possible. But it is no less true that
man's distinctive shame lies in the fact that the extent of his
sympathy, vast though it is, is so much less than it might be.
For, while a Christ will possess a flame of active sympathy
for all humanity and a Buddha a passive sympathy for all
sentient beings, most of us restrict our sympathies to those
bound up with us by ties of propinquity or homogeneity.
Neighborhood, nation or class, family, and race or species
in varying degrees, afford a basis for altruistic regard. But all
too often it seems impossible to make people's sympathies
extend to more than a fraction of one or a few of these cultural domains. There are so many who limit in some cruel and
arbitrary way their concern for others. Consider the attitudes
of the orthodox to the heterodox, of the white to the colored,
of the nationalist to the alien, of the greedy exploiter to his
tenants or hirelings, of the Nazi 'Aryan' to Jews and liberals,

of the Bolshevik proletarian to members of another class or even of another revolutionary party, and last, but by no means least, the incredible lack of feeling on the part of the majority of human beings for the animals whose mental inferiority and helplessness at our hands should elicit from us a very special and chivalric pity. It is curious as well as sad that this sympathy, which is the loveliest of the virtues and which in some of us shines brightly in some directions, can be so easily deadened or dimmed in other directions by the blindness of prejudice." [2]

Selfishness seems to be a fundamental cause of all evils. Evil arises from the attempt of men to gain more than their proper proportion of satisfactions. Untruthfulness, theft, murder, rape, adultery, injustice are also selfish acts. Acts of selfishness are those in which men treat themselves as privileged persons or as special cases. "The root of all selfishness, and indeed in the end the root of all evil, lies in the fact that each man tends to prefer himself simply because he is himself, and apart from any question of needs or deserts or any other circumstances. . . . No one can claim *privilege,* none can claim that, apart from special superiorities in his deserts, his abilities, or his circumstances, he is entitled to more consideration than other people. The equality of all men before the law is thus the juridical expression of the philosophical principle of the intrinsic equality of all persons as persons." [3]

Group selfishness is a very dangerous kind of selfishness because it so often masquerades under the cloak of loyalty to some cause. When men join groups and institutions they tend to come under a new and different set of loyalties or allegiances. They may come to see things from a special point of view or in segments, and they may form attitudes and perform deeds as members of the group which the individuals, or many of them, would not do alone. A member of a family in his desire to promote its welfare may act contrary to the interests of the community. A member of a labor union may carry out some act with a sense of satisfaction that he is serving his group. His act may be detrimental to the interest of society, but he does not look at it from that point of view. The same type of action may be performed by the business executive, or the member of a lodge. A high morality attempts to help men to see the wider implications of their acts and to form judgments or to make decisions from the point of view of the larger whole. Stated in another way, men are morally mature only when they learn to find their happiness in ways that make happiness possible for all men and women.

In sociological literature a distinction is made between groups that is fruitful in helping us to understand this problem of individual and group selfishness. The distinction is that of the "in-group" and the "out-group" which enables us to explain how one may love and hate at the same time. We may have sympathy, affection, and loyalty for the members of our own group, the in-group, while holding an attitude of hatred, avoidance, and suspicion for the members of the out-group.

The in-group, out-group relationship does not remain constant throughout life. Much depends upon the tensions and strains within a given society. The in-group may be the family, the gang or club, or one's church. Let a split come within one of these groups and our side becomes the in-group. When we are thinking politically, the nation is usually the in-group, but during war it may become for a time a group of allied nations. Today the world is divided and subdivided into areas of suspicion, hatred, and conflict. All too frequently the church, instead of leading the way to a world-wide fellowship, has produced individual Christians who are decent and even "pious" and loving in a narrow sense, but who are really "pagans" in their social and international outlook.

A considerable part of the chaos, the despair, the violence, and the general immorality of the modern world is due to the fact that we do not recognize the sacredness of persons and the common humanity of all men. If we are to be mature, our moral outlook must transcend the barriers of class, religious denomination, nation, color, and race. We are morally mature only when for us the in-group includes humanity.

The demands both of a mature morality and of high religion are for a true community which will enable us to place humanity above class, nationality, and race. Christianity, where true to its ideal, gives men a frame of reference outside and beyond themselves and their narrow group relationships. A world-wide Christian fellowship has been developing. Stimulated by the Oxford, Edinburgh, and the Madras Conferences in which representatives from most nations were present, a beginning has been made toward a world organization of Christians. A world fellowship in which all men regard the interests of their fellows as of equal value with their own is the distant goal. Such a movement needs support and encouragement.

III. *A Mature Morality is one which places a premium upon knowledge and intelligence.*

In considering the marks of a mature morality we pointed out, first, that we judge an act on the basis of its effect upon persons or human welfare. But this requires knowledge and understanding of the nature of man, of human society, and of the nature of the universe. We also pointed out, in the

second place, that love and a spirit of unselfishness are also
moral demands. But if men are to do to others as they would
have others do to them, they must be able to know and to
appreciate sympathetically just what they would be likely to
want done to them if they were actually in the other person's place and circumstances. Unless this is to some extent
possible, an emphasis on altruism may be mere pious sentiment.

In modern society it appears that we cannot be "good"
unless we are also informed and intelligent. Goodness alone
is not enough. To choose the right course of action in any
genuinely moral sense, we must know what is the right course
of action. Saintliness or individual piety alone is no guarantee
of vision or wisdom in either individual action or social policy. The "saints" are found on both sides of controversial
questions. Men have given their best efforts for the losing side
of issues which are now agreed upon and settled. One's conscience may be an unsafe guide unless it is significantly informed by the facts of the situation and by reflection on moral
issues. Conscience, as the late Canon Streeter has reminded
us, is very definitely "not a 'labor-saving' device" to save us
from the trouble of carefully thinking things through.[4]

In one of his essays, John Erskine points out that there is
an old Anglo-Saxon tradition that intelligence is often a
danger, and that goodness is the important thing. The prov-
erb: "Be good, sweet maid, and let who will be clever," seems
to imply that a choice must be made between goodness and
intelligence. If people have thought there was a conflict or a
separation then we ought to demand "union now." Neither
good intentions alone, nor intelligence alone, will suffice. Some
of the great tragedies of the past and of the present are due
not just to vicious intent, but to a lack of knowledge and of
"thinking." At other times, when we think we are thinking,

our judgments are warped by our special interests and by our prejudices. "Thinking," said Voltaire, "is so difficult; that is why most of us prefer to pass judgments."

While we are all human and make mistakes, and while we cannot hold a person responsible for unavoidable ignorance, it is the duty of all morally earnest persons to be as significantly informed and as wise as possible. A man may have the best of intentions and yet bring great harm and tragedy if he has not also taken the trouble or the care to be informed. Sometimes it is all too true that "the road to hell is paved with good intentions." The doctor who fails to follow the latest developments in his field may be the cause of a patient's death as surely as if he had neglected him. The engineer who fails to check details carefully and to use available information may be the cause of injury and loss of life. The missionary who is a narrow individualist, a bigoted nationalist, and devoid of a knowledge of psychology and sociology may do as much harm as he does good. The reader will think of many other examples. In the course of her lectures, during a tour of America a few years ago, Miss Muriel Lester of England said in effect that she did not know which had done the greater harm in the world, the good men who lacked intelligence, or the intelligent men who lacked character. One of the statesmen, she went on to say, who was more responsible than others in England for some of the acts which led to the first World War, was a devout Christian man, from the traditional point of view, who went to church every morning before breakfast. The hope of the future must rest on the willingness of persons of good intention to form their opinions on the basis of evidence, rather than upon sentiment, tradition, and prejudice.

In a complex society, where men wield great power and where their actions may affect the lives of other persons, public welfare may be endangered as much by ignorance and carelessness as by willful aggression. Since this is the case, a sensitive and morally mature person will endeavor to make himself as well informed as possible, not only about his own work or profession, but about the possible effect of his actions on all other persons.

During recent decades there has been a tendency for students of man to emphasize his animal ancestry and to glorify either instinct or conditioned reflexes. Unconscious rather than conscious motivations have been emphasized. Factors of the physical, biological, and social environments have been used to explain man's reactions and general behavior. Increasing mechanization and mass production in society, with less chance for originality and independence for many persons, made it easier to believe that perhaps the world, too, was a mechanism or that there was some pre-determined pattern of life. These trends in interpretation seemed to receive some support from the outbreak of the World War, 1914-1918, by the present world conflict, and by the rise of a new barbarism.

During the same period an army of specialists entered the various sciences. They gave their undivided attention to highly specialized fields of research, with little or no thought and attention to morals, to social philosophy, or to the application of their special knowledge. Their attitude of objectivity and detachment has frequently led to an irresponsible attitude toward the world, and to a failure to understand what is happening in society. The result too frequently has been an exclusive trust in science with a denial of whatever lies beyond the reach of objective methods, a distrust of any cause and any statement of principles, and a failure to defend the world by which they live. While specialization brings benefits that cannot be denied, it may lead men to see life in fragments and so to trivialize and to confuse the human intellect.

While the eighteenth century and the "Age of Reason"

may have gone too far in emphasizing reason to the exclusion of the non-rational elements in man's life, our age may be giving too much emphasis to the non-rational elements. After long ages of development, man has risen to the point where he may live to some extent on the level of intelligence and conscious choice. The aim or the hope for the future is that he may increasingly substitute intelligence for chance or passion in the conduct of his life and that of society. In speaking of the "spiritual decadence in mankind," Albert Schweitzer tells us that he is in complete disagreement with the spirit of the age because it is permeated with disdain for thinking or reflection. Such an attitude is an indication of spiritual bankruptcy. When men cease to believe that they can discover the truth by their own thinking, skepticism is the result. He considers it a part of his mission and work to make people think.[5]

Men need discipline and balance if their emotions and appetites are not to run away with them. This necessitates the guidance of intelligence. More than two thousand years ago, Plato divided the life of man into three parts. There was a desiring part located in the abdomen. This is the seat of man's passions and appetites. Since there is no principle of order or harmony here, this part needs to be brought under the control of reason. There was a feeling part located in the breast. It was the basis of the heroic virtues. There was a rational part located in the head or brain. The mind, by a sort of divine right, was destined to rule the other parts, and this was the case in the mature and harmonious life. His study of the psychological nature of man led Plato to set forth three natural groupings in the state or in society. The workers, corresponding to the appetites in man, were to furnish the material foundations of the state. Their virtue is self-control. The officials and warriors, corresponding to the feelings in man, were to execute the laws and to guard the state. Their virtue is courage. The intellectuals, the rulers, corresponding to the reason in man, were to rule the state in the interest of the common good. Their virtue is wisdom. Only as all these parts functioned harmoniously would there be justice. While we may not be able to follow all the details of Plato's psychology and social philosophy, his emphasis upon the importance of intelligence is instructive. Intelligence is not opposed to the senses or to the emotions; it is rather, their harmonizer. Whereas the senses tend to emphasize the here and now or the immediate present, man's rational nature surveys the past and the future and tends to evaluate the part in the light of the larger whole. In this way it ordinarily gives a more balanced or sane perspective.

Emotional adulthood is the ability to stand up to each new situation as it really is, to face the facts, and to make the best adjustment that appears possible under the circumstances. Life is such that none of us can satisfy all our desires. When our emotions are frustrated we may blame others, get angry, attempt to escape through hysteria or other means. To face the facts and make a wise adjustment requires intelligence. A mature morality must grasp clearly the significance and importance of knowledge and intelligence. To choose the right, one must know what is right under the circumstances. The quest for truth must go along with purposeful living.

When faced with a moral problem the intelligent man will attempt to discover and to weigh all the relevant factors in the situation. The more he knows about the world in which he lives, and about life and its relationships, the more likely is he to be able to decide wisely. He will consider past experience as well as present circumstances, since moral principles are tested in part by racial experience. He will want to judge by the years and the centuries, not by the impulses of the moment. Moreover, he will need to consider the possible future, what he wants to become and what he hopes to achieve. This approach places a premium upon knowledge and emphasizes the need of constructive or creative intelligence.

IV. *We are Morally Mature only when we rely on inner rather than upon outer controls.*

In the midst of a rising tide of compulsion and force in the world, men need to realize more clearly than ever before that character cannot be forced. If men do things merely because of social pressure, or custom, or fear, or the law, they are not in the highest sense moral. In a world of increasing complexity we shall probably need more and more regulation and planning so that we may go ahead in an orderly way and with greater safety. Yet we do need to remember that good will cannot be compelled. Christian ethics is an ethics of the spirit, inner and free, the very antithesis of legalism, externalism, and authoritarianism.

In modern society there is a deepening conflict between the area of voluntariness or freedom and the area of coercion. Whenever coercion increases, it means that voluntariness has failed. If there are not enough volunteers, there must be conscripts. If men fail to do what is right, there must be laws to restrain them from wrong-doing. We are going to have more voluntary free life, or we are going to have more coercion and conscription. Unless we can have more uncompelled good will and more uncompelled strength of character, the amount of external coercion is likely to grow.

A nineteenth century moral philosopher, T. H. Green, tells us that "that man is free who is conscious of being the author of the law that he obeys." If the law is my law then I am free. If it is imposed upon me from the outside, then I am not free. An ideal society would be one in which each person agrees to every law that is passed and thinks of it as a part of his own desire and will. Since this ideal is not attained, the next best thing is to permit those who do not agree to criticize and to agitate for something different. Freedom may be a more severe master than the law because it demands the education of the person in self-discipline, a deepening of the sense of responsibility, resistance against subjection to passing moods, and the development of loyalty and patience. These, however, are elements of all higher cultures as well as of a mature morality.

A unique service of the Hebrew prophets was to lead men in their search for the good life and for God away from external things to their own inner lives. Two lines of development are important to note in this connection. The first is the emergence of the individual and the recognition of individual responsibility. When the Hebrew people first entered Palestine, the family or group was the important unit. If one member of a family committed an offense, then the whole group was punished. When Achan sinned, not only Achan, but his kin and all his possessions were destroyed. At a later time Ezekiel says: "The soul that sinneth, it shall die. The son shall not bear the iniquity of the father, neither shall the father bear the iniquity of the son." A second development is away from an emphasis upon ritual and outward conformity to personal purity and sincerity within. "Man looketh on the outward appearance, but the Lord looketh on the heart." "What doth the Lord require of thee, but to do justly, and to love mercy, and to walk humbly with thy God."

Jesus carried forward this same emphasis. He stressed the fundamental inwardness of morality. Emphasis was placed on the state of man's feeling, will, and thought, as well as upon conditions in the world at large. Jesus took the earlier commandments and interpreted them from the standpoint of their inner attitude. "You have heard that it was said to them of old time, thou shalt not kill; and whosoever shall kill shall be in danger of the judgment; but I say unto you, that every one who is angry with his brother, without a cause, shall be in danger of the judgment; and whosoever shall say to his brother, Raca, shall be in danger of the council; and whosoever shall say: Thou fool, shall be in danger of the fire of hell." In the Sermon on the Mount, Jesus commended the "poor in spirit," "the meek," "the merciful," "the pure in heart," "they that hunger and thirst after righteousness."

Paul the Apostle saw clearly that outward conformity is not enough. "Though I bestow all my goods to feed the poor . . . and have not love, it profiteth me nothing." He was an outstanding exponent of self-discipline, and self-control. His life and his teachings conform in this respect. "I bring my body into subjection, all my powers into control, and am temperate in all things." "Every man that striveth in the games exerciseth self-control in all things."

For moral maturity there must be that personal self-discipline which makes a man's conduct distinctly his own. Probably more men go down in life's struggle because they have failed to master themselves than for any other reason. Life needs to be governed from within on the basis of an ethical ideal or a philosophy of life that has been consciously accepted. Aristotle, when asked what good his philosophy did him, is said to have replied that because of it he did voluntarily what most other men did only for fear of the law. Kant insisted that when man obeys the sense of duty within himself, or the moral law, he governs himself. Moral autonomy is needed if man is to be free. Mark Twain felt that honor was a sterner master than the law.

This self-discipline and inner control must include a sense of responsibility for one's actions and the effects of one's deeds.

At times this will include the acceptance or acknowledgement of blame or guilt. Above all we need to avoid easy rationalizations and exception-making and the tendency to project blame upon others. The mature man faces facts and reality in his own life as well as in his world. Men are expected not only to "do right" but to "be good." Hypocrisy is grossly immoral. A mature morality stresses character as well as conduct. The springs of action, the motive, the intention, the spirit, are as important as the overt conduct. Mere formalism and conformity are not in the highest sense moral.

V. *A Mature Morality judges the entire act, which includes a motive or motives, means, and consequences.*

Conduct ordinarily begins with desire growing out of some need. The dominant desire is called the *motive* or intention of the act. The emphasis in the previous section, upon inner control rather than upon mere outer conformity, may imply in the minds of some that motive alone is the important thing. However, there are other things which are also important in judging human conduct. There may be various *means* or ways by which we can attain the end or goal which we have in mind, and in addition to this, the act will have certain general *consequences* or effects upon persons and social groups.

In the past various theories of morality have tended to stress the first part or the last part of the act. For example, Immanuel Kant, 1724–1804, emphasized a good motive, or a good will. "Nothing can possibly be conceived in the world, or even out of it, which can be called good without qualification, except a good will." He thinks there is no direct connection between the morality of an act and its effects. If a man acts from a good motive, or out of loyalty to a sense of duty,

the act is good regardless of its consequences. Kant does not
say that effects are unimportant, but merely that the moral
quality of the act is not determined by them.

On the other hand, for Jeremy Bentham, 1748–1832, and
John Stuart Mill, 1806–1873, two outstanding Utilitarians,
consequences are the important parts of action and they determine whether an act is right or wrong. An action is not to
be called right or wrong because it is performed by a good
or a bad man. Such considerations, they assert, are important
in the estimations of persons but not of actions. A right act
is an act that leads to desirable results. Actions are right as
they tend to promote happiness, wrong as they tend to produce
pain. A further elaboration of the various theories which emphasize consequences will not be attempted.

Interpretations of morality which stress motives alone, or
those which stress consequences alone, seem to me to be one-
sided and fallacious. There is no part of the entire process,
motive, means, and consequences which can be ignored without danger. Let us consider each part briefly. Motives are
important, even basic, for morality. A good motive is a pre-
requisite to conduct which we wholeheartedly approve. If a
good intention is lacking, the act, even though beneficial, is
either not approved, or is approved with reservations. If a
good motive is absent, we know that the good consequences
occurred in spite of his intentions or because of circumstances
which he either did not understand or could not foresee. We
cannot feel kindly toward such a one. If a good motive is
present and the act leads to harmful effects, we tend to condemn less severely or to excuse the person by saying: "At least
his intentions were good."

Motives are not everything, however. When a man earnestly
asks, "What is right in this situation?" and we reply by telling

him to have a good motive, we do not meet his problem. In order to do right, he must discover what is right. The question assumes that his intention is to do what is right if he can find the way. Granted that the man has a good motive and is morally responsible, what ought he to do in circumstances such as are before him? Good will does not express itself in a social vacuum. In order to do our duty we must know what is our duty. To do the Will of God we must discover what His Will is in the situation at hand. A mature man needs to analyze not only the motives which prompt him to act, but also the situation in which his actions will take place. We are led, therefore, to examine means and consequences of our acts.

We must employ some means or our intention will not be carried out. Just as there may be many motives for performing an act, there may be various means or ways of reaching our goal. Once chosen, however, the means become part of the general act and part of our intention. The means used may be morally neutral. Whether I walk or ride, providing I can keep my appointment, may not involve a question of right or wrong. The means used to attain some good end may be wrong, such as selling "dope" to support one's family. Or these means may be admirable or right. Ordinarily, we expect a man to use the best means available to accomplish his purpose. Good consequences can be achieved only by the use of appropriate means. The means may determine the nature of the results to be attained.

Consequences are also important. We expect the general consequences of an act we call right to be good or beneficial to the persons involved. When a man asks, "What is right?" he is usually thinking of consequences. What course of action will bring the greatest happiness or well-being or will lead to the highest development of personality? Yet consequences are not everything, as we have seen. We may approve the surgical operation which turns out disastrously. The intention was good and there was at least the possibility that the consequences might have been good.

Conduct is right if it proceeds from a noble or praiseworthy motive, through the use of good means, to effects that are beneficial. Let any one of these conditions be violated, and men will approve of the conduct with reservations or they will condemn the action.

VI. *A Mature Morality recognizes that for a better society we need both transformed individuals and social reconstruction.*

For the early Christians, the "good news" was that salvation was possible, but Christians have never entirely agreed as to how the world was to be saved. Is it by "faith" only, or by "good works" alone? Is it by conversion of the individual or is it by the transformation of the social order?

The same issue has arisen between groups that are not directly motivated by religion. The individualist tells us that our social programs are ineffective, if not positively damaging. Ability and character will succeed under any circumstances. Not social control nor social reconstruction, but individual initiative and freedom are stressed. This makes men and women of us, he says, while paternalistic social programs will sap our vitality and aggressiveness.

In modern Christianity the issue has expressed itself as a conflict between the way of personal evangelism and the social gospel. "Only saved individuals can save society" says one; "Only in a saved society can men remain saved," is the reply. Let us consider these contentions in turn.

I

Some educators, religious leaders, business men, and others, contend or assume that the trouble with our society is merely that, as individuals, we are selfish or sinful. They say that if we improve or transform individuals, a good society will be the result and our problem will be solved in this way.

There is some truth in this position. Our individual lives are of primary importance. There can be no love, friendliness, and happiness that are not the love, friendliness, and happiness of individual persons. We cannot have a good society made up of vicious depraved individuals. Selfish, dishonest, narrow individuals will ruin any system.

Again, we shall always have private problems to face in any society, and these will need personal attention. Suffering, personal and mental, maladjustment and disorders of various kinds are likely to occur in any society that we can foresee. The problem of generating morale, moral courage, and insight, as well as a change of heart and purpose will ever be present. Principal John S. Whale, of Cheshunt College, Cambridge, has put this truth forcefully: "The world is wrong, not because it has not yet discovered a new social technique, but because individual hearts are wrong. Sin would still be our stark intractable problem if we all woke to find ourselves in Utopia tomorrow morning. Problems innumerable wait for their solution at the hands of statesmen, scientists, economists, and teachers; but there is not a social problem under heaven which can advance toward real solution unless the greater problem of which it is an aspect is first met and dealt with in the secret places of the individual heart. It is there that the solution must be found if it is to be found at all. Only redemption and conversion can meet our case. . . . The causes of the folly and woe of our time and of all times do not lie exclusively

in vast intangibles such as the Economic System or the National
System, but in me and others everywhere like me who make
the systems what they are. I find that my failure, my greed,
my fear, match yours and that our lives interlock to form an
organized system of evil." [6]

Nevertheless, while "saved" individuals are an essential of
a good society, it is well to keep in mind that our private lives
are not the only ones we live. Men are part of a collective public life and of institutions which mold their lives in subtle
ways. The person inevitably suffers when the public life of
which he is a part is far behind his personal standards. While
he is waiting to reform enough individuals, great collective
maladjustments may lead to disaster. While he is winning
individuals one by one, the social order may be demoralizing
them by the score.

Realizing that in evangelism men ought not to ignore the
need for changing social institutions and patterns, the Madras
Conference of Christians declared: "It is not enough to say
that if we change the individual we will of necessity change
the social order. This is a half truth. For the social order is
not entirely made up of individuals now living. It is made up
of inherited attitudes which have come down from generation
to generation through customs, laws, institutions, and these
exist in large measure independently of individuals now living.
Change those individuals and you do not of necessity change
the social order unless you organize those changed individuals
into collective action on a wide-scale, frontal attack upon these
corporate evils." [7]

2

Over against the belief that our one main task is to transform individuals is the belief that all we need to do is to
change the structure of society and all our problems will be

near solution. From the time of Plato and Aristotle to the
modern communists and others, men have declared that a good
society, or social and economic reconstruction, is necessary
for the production of good men.

There is considerable truth in this position. In the first
place, a society must enable its members to live and to fulfill
the normal functions of the life cycle or there would be no
individuals to transform. In the second place, institutions and
programs tend to create men of a certain type or character,
and institutions may be judged in considerable part by the
kind of men they produce. Human nature is not some constant, static things which persists in the same form under
any and every condition. To do things in one way may produce a certain kind of person. To do things another way
may produce another kind of person.

The institutions under which men live and work may pre-
dispose them to selfishness or to social service. A society which
emphasizes self-interest, competition, and individualism leads
to the prevalence of war, labor disputes, vigilantism, and the
like. A social system that emphasizes co-operation, social welfare, and intelligent planning might make the development
of noble individuals possible where it is exceedingly difficult
today.

While persons in the high stages of spiritual development
may overcome adverse circumstances, this is not true of
children nor of average men and women. The assumption
that the person can develop his highest possibilities or capabilities apart from external circumstances is false. The denial
of advantages on the social and economic level frequently
means the denial of privileges on the spiritual level. Boys
engaged in street trades are ten times more likely to become
delinquent than boys brought up in the normal home-school
relationships. A playground and a program of organized

recreation have been found to eliminate delinquency from some areas where delinquency has been prevalent. There is a close relationship between crime, and hence probably of character, on the one hand, and economic status, occupation, and location in a city, et cetera, on the other hand.

Writing in the *Journal of Philosophy,* H. C. Brown says: "The most disturbing feature of this moral picture is the extent to which so many well-disposed people have been misled to believe that the remedy for our ills lies in sound moral training in the home or the school, or that the authority of religion can adequately form character. In reality, the pressures to which a young man or woman is subjected when he or she attempts to find a place in the world of economic competition, are infinitely stronger and more persistent educative forces than home, school, or church." [8]

The tragic inability of Christianity to prevent the national and international debacle in which modern civilization finds itself may be due, in part, to the fact that large sections of the Christian church are teaching men to think individually as Christians, but are failing to teach them to apply their principles to the social and national orders. Consequently, these individual Christians may be narrow and unchristian in so far as their social and international thinking and attitudes are concerned.

In our moral and religious thinking we may commit the logical "fallacy of composition" by assuming that a whole is simply the sum of its parts. On the contrary, there are qualities in wholes or in totalities which are not found in the parts separately. Just as water has a quality which is not found in the hydrogen and oxygen that make up its parts, so life has a quality not found in the physical and chemical units of which it is composed. Because all the members of a committee are experts in their individual fields does not necessarily mean that the action of the committee will be highly intelligent. Transforming the individuals does not necessarily mean that the society of which the individuals are a part will be transformed. Individual salvation may remain individual and have little effect unless the implications of the new way of life for social or economic or international life are made clear. If organizations, institutions, and groups are wholes which are distinct from the sum of their individual parts, then attention must be given to those wholes as well as to the parts. A good motive, piety, and saintliness, do not necessarily mean that men will have vision and wisdom in social action.

A re-examination of the life of Jesus in the light of this problem is illuminating. Salvation for Jesus was both a social and an individual affair. He gave attention to men's motives and attitudes, but he also gave attention to the conditions under which they lived. The task of healing, feeding, and clothing them was part of his mission. Salvation was a matter of saving others as well as a personal problem. He was interested in men's social and economic salvation because he seemed to realize that it was a part of the process of saving individual men.

While we must attempt to transform society, to make this the whole or single task would be absurd. The Madras Conference reports, after showing the need of changing society as quoted above, go on to say: "While it is a half truth to say that changed individuals will necessarily change the social order, it is also a half truth to say that social change will necessarily produce individual change. We cannot sustain a new social order or bring it into being without new men. For in the ultimate analysis the whole outer structure of society rests upon human character." [9]

Individual reformation or regeneration and social reconstruction must go hand in hand. There may be times, when social tension and maladjustment are at a minimum, when the problem of individual transformation may seem more important. There may be other periods when men are impressed by the urgent need of some great reform in the social order. In such situations, they should attempt to bring to bear upon these problems an informed moral judgment. No condition ought to be tolerated that makes the regeneration of individuals difficult. At all times, however, the church must build a social conscience that hates both individual sins and social evils.

VII. *We are Morally Mature only when we are willing to grow along with the growing, changing world.*

Growth is one of the first laws of life. For persons this growth is not only physical but intellectual, emotional, and cultural. A person's mental age, commonly referred to as his I.Q. or intelligence quotient, his emotional age, even his social and cultural maturity, are often distinguished from his physical or chronological age. A fourteen-year-old boy might have a mental age of eighteen, an educational age of the average sixteen-year-old boy, but only an emotional age of the normal ten-year-old. For a person to be and to remain mature is more difficult, in a rapidly changing society, where we are called upon to deal with many new situations, and where older behavior patterns are often inadequate. In a mobile social order we need to strive continuously to be significantly informed, to maintain a flexibility of mind, and to acquire the desire and the ability to deal realistically with persons and with things.

While there are many persons who are immature intellectually, there are probably more who are emotionally immature. Growth in this phase of life will be indicated by an increasing ability to stand up to each new situation, as it really is, and to react to it adequately, unhampered by infantile emotional habits. The process of "weaning" needs to go on right through life. The infant gets emotional satisfaction from sucking, but at a certain age that practice must be left behind. We say the child is weaned. Weaning is giving up some habit, highly charged with emotion, for a more mature or adequate one. At a later age the boy or girl must be able to give up dependence upon parents and home, and parents must be willing to permit their children to face life for themselves. New emotional patterns need to be built from infancy to old age if we are to become emotionally mature. We must grow by the things we give up as well as by the new powers and insights we achieve.

Life is such that none of us can satisfy all our desires all the time. What do we do when our desires and emotions are blocked? The immature person is likely to blame others for his difficulties. He may shift responsibility for his deeds to other persons or things. He may find excuses or rationalizations, not the real reasons, or he may easily deceive himself or others. In contrast to this, the person who has grown emotionally, and is more mature, attempts to face realities and to make his decisions on the basis of an examination of the facts as nearly as he can discover them. He is able to discuss disputed issues without getting angry or emotionally wrought up. He can hold strong convictions without being dogmatic. He is conscious of his deficiencies and is able to profit by criticism. Ability to take criticism is an evidence of emotional maturity.

We grow as we respond to the worthwhile things in our environment. I have heard it said that the frog is so easily adapted to its environment and so unconscious of slight changes that if it is put in a pan of water and the water slowly heated the frog will stay there until it is boiled alive although it could have jumped out at any moment. Many people are much like frogs. Changes in the environment, in living conditions, and in ideas are imperceptible to them. Their minds die instead of becoming alert to meet the newer conditions. When society changes, we need to change constructively and to grow, or the unity of our lives may be broken and we may become confused or frustrated.

Man lives in a world that beckons him toward innumerable rich and meaningful relationships in the fields of art, science, philosophy, and religion. He needs to cultivate the rich overtones of life, to find his aptitudes, to develop his interests, and to press on toward new and rewarding frontiers of life. Satisfaction and joy come from an inward hospitality to truth, beauty, and goodness in their many forms. Intimate and frequent contact with the highest and the best in one's environment is essential to a growing, serene, and well-balanced life.

If men are growing themselves and if they live in an evolving, changing world, morality cannot be static. Since life is a growth, moral codes, if they are to retain their appeal, must be progressive and dynamic. As new conditions arise, and as new insights present themselves, moral codes must grow and expand to meet the new circumstances. Morality is not something artificial and apart; it grows out of the conditions of life itself.

An examination of the past will indicate, as we have seen in an earlier chapter, that morality, like our language and our bodies, is the product of a long period of development and adaptation. Moral standards vary from the customs of primitive man, who was only partly conscious of what was taking place, to the reasoned theories of life of some modern men. Even today we find men living at all stages of moral evolution. Mature morality is a gradual process of development in the individual and in the race.

During early times the authority of custom or of the group was powerful. Since the time of the Renaissance and the Reformation, however, the reign of authority has been growing weaker. Large numbers of persons have become dissatisfied with the older authorities. Some have failed to discover the new basis for conduct and they are confused and often indifferent or even antagonistic to all standards. An increasing number are attempting to distinguish between right and wrong on the basis of an application of intelligence to the facts of life and of human progress. They believe that it is possible to do consciously and more intelligently what has been going on in a haphazard and confused way in the past. An examination of the past will reveal the slow adaptation of moral ideas and practices to the needs of men under the conditions in which they lived. In the past there has been growth through experimentation even though it has been only partly conscious and ill directed.

We cannot expect to arrive or to say the last word in an evolving universe. If life is a growth, the moral codes of the present must be left open for the contributions of the future. Many of the supposed "finalities" and "certainties" of the past have turned out to be uncertainties, and some of them to be entirely false. If we cannot be absolutely certain, we can be reasonably certain. Moreover, we can gain a sense of progress and the thrill of creativity. We can play the game fairly as we understand it and also assist in its improvement.

Our attitude must be dynamic and creative. The conditions and experiences of life appear to justify this attitude rather than one which assumes a static or fixed universe. When men cease to think of the world as fixed and think of it as a growth which is amenable to human control, they approach it with a different attitude. If men earnestly believe that they live in a world that can be made better, they will probably live in a better world than they would have otherwise, because they are more likely to do something about it.

As men discover better ways of living and working, the older ways tend to become "evil." As men come to view evil as that which ought to be eliminated, and as they come to feel an obligation to co-operate with other men to right the wrongs that exist, they will discover a new sense of the meaning and joy of living. One of the main tasks of our age is to produce men and women who will have both the knowledge and the desire to take the products of human invention and use them so that they will create, not destruction and tragedy, but personality and social welfare.

VIII. *A Mature Morality interprets our human duties as duties to God and thus it gives cosmic significance to the moral life.*

There are moralists who like to maintain that morality is independent of religion and that the good life has value in its own right. There is some truth in this position. Morality rests on present facts and realities. Right is right because it is intrinsically valuable to persons. "Thou shalt not steal" is good morals quite apart from any supernatural authority and under any system of ethics, religious or secular, Christian or non-Christian. We are interested, however, in the deepest and most adequate interpretation of the facts which life presents. When men cut themselves off from religion and from belief in God the effect is more likely to be expressed in terms of a lowered morale or enthusiasm about life. Sometimes, however, they do become completely demoralized.

Many of the religious humanists claim that man is the highest product of the creative process and that there is nothing above or beyond him but his own ideals. The universe, they say, is indifferent toward the human enterprise and men should acknowledge this fact. They fear that theism draws off interest and energy from human values and centers them in another world, whereas they ought to be centered directly upon men's achievable ideals.

That religion has sometimes been used as a means of escape from present tasks and problems is undoubtedly true. That does not necessarily lead to an indictment of all religion. We shall consider this question more fully in a later chapter entitled Religion, Ethical and Unethical. Questions of morality cannot be separated permanently from questions as to the nature of man and of the universe, as we have seen. What man ought to do depends upon what he is, and upon his place in the larger scheme of things. A man's convictions about the meaning of the world will affect his spirit and outlook and hence his conduct. Moreover, the origin of what is distinctive in man reaches back into his organic or biological nature. Organic nature, in turn, reaches back into the nature of the universe. Man seems to be a genuine product of the creative processes of the universe. To separate him too completely from them seems unreasonable.

Interpretations of man which make him a mere animal, a mere mechanism or physiological process, a mere producer or consumer, are only half truths. The self is more than a thing of nature. While man is electronic, and atomic, and cellular, he is more than these. He is a self, an "I," that transcends all these parts of which he is composed. As a self, man is free to some extent from the limitations of these other levels of existence. As a personality, he lives not only in a realm that is chemical and physical, but also in a realm that is rational and ethical.

Not only is man a self, a personality, but there is in him a creative urge that is a part of, or related to, the creative forces of the universe. At times it expresses itself as desire, interest, instinct, or will. At other times it is manifest in thinking and it wells up in conscious life. It expresses itself in the creative achievements of science, art, philosophy, and religion. In the universe there exists a creativity, a spirit that leads in the direction of truth, beauty, goodness, and the development of persons. There must be personality-producing forces in the universe or it would not have produced man. If we are to live wholesome lives, to gain unity and meaning, we must relate our lives to that in the universe which is creating personality and goodness.

In the high levels of moral decision and action, men feel that the call of duty comes from beyond their isolated selves. "There is a mystical aspect in our highest moral moments." Life overflows all that can be said in interpretation of it. The meaning, the significance, and the richness of life transcends its descriptions and concepts. Theism is an interpretation of the universe which makes it possible for man to believe in a cosmic support of his ideals and values.

Stated in religious terms, man is conscious of fellowship with God and reinforcement from Him. Part of the aim of Jesus was to make clear that God's nature is such, and man's nature is such, that there can be an intimate fellowship between God and man. Christian morality is distinctive in interpreting the duties of man as duties to God. Thus religion and morality are brought together as integral to human nature. Whereas secular ethics is likely to talk about the highest good, the Christian is likely to talk also about the Will of God.

Men discover empirically or through experience the tasks which need to be done; then these tasks are viewed as a part of their duty to God. This leaves to man the task of discovering, or the decision, as to what is right in the particular situation. Men are inspired by their religion and love of God to discover the right and to walk according to it. Religion is thus seen as a powerful motivation directing men's lives in the way they should go, rather than indicating the particular acts they should perform.

In Christian morality, to live the good life is obedience to God. The highest morality springs from a new relation to God. The right may be stated in terms of loyalty to Christ. Jesus Christ is taken as the embodiment of the ideal and loyalty to him means loyalty to the best possible life in the situation in which men find themselves. The Christian life is a quest for the good under the inspiration of devotion to the ideals of Jesus. Thus the moral appeal is personalized through its identification with Jesus, and through him, with God. The influence of a person is stronger than that of a concept. The power of a great personality who lived out his ideals reinforces the ideals of men. Christianity ties ethics to a religious world view and gives the moral life cosmic significance. Belief is reinforced by experience that in Christianity men have the highest stimulus to high living. If, as we believe, an immanent God works through the nature which has produced man, and if it is possible for man to commune with God and to receive support for his highest endeavors, then man must recognize this fact and co-operate in order to live his life at its highest and best.

CHAPTER V

COMPROMISE AND EXPERIMENTATION

THERE ARE TWO very important questions which modern
men are asking and which are ignored too frequently in
discussions of both general ethics and Christian ethics.
First, in a mature morality is there any place for compromise,
or does compromise always imply that one is selecting a lower
good, if not some definite evil? Second, how are we to adapt
our codes and our conduct to the new problems and situations
in life? Is experimentation, the method which has been so
fruitful in other fields, applicable to the realm of morality?
In this chapter we shall consider both of these questions.

Compromise

In actual life there is often a great distance between our
ideal, the way which we firmly believe to be the best, and the
thing which seems to be possible under the circumstances. If
we cannot do the ideal thing, how are we to determine what
course to pursue? Should an agreement ever be broken? Are
there conditions under which a promise, a contract, or a
treaty may be rightly broken? Are there exceptions, or is the
duty of carrying out the letter of an agreement an absolute
one? Is there any place for compromise in the Christian outlook and way of life? [1]

1. Types of Compromise

The attitude of compromise, or of laxity toward some agreement or some standard, is likely to be morally suspect. Under

certain conditions it is clearly wrong. This is the case when we deviate from some clear moral demand and give way to the indulgence of some personal desire which has no genuine claim against that demand. Whether we give way completely or stop at some half-way point between the two, the compromise is to be condemned. To "split the difference" between a line of duty and some vice is clearly to err. In this sense compromise is an indication of indifference or cowardice or a moral laxity that may approach gross immorality. Nor are we likely to have respect for the person who lightly casts aside his ideas and ideals merely because those about him do not accept them. To pretend to accept the misconceptions and false ideas of others is to give way to hypocrisy. Our repugnance to these types of compromise is likely to carry over and make it easy for us to condemn all compromise, regardless of its nature. There are, however, other types of compromise.

The situation is quite different when the problem is a choice between two conflicting duties. Abraham was forced to choose between devotion to a tribal religious rite and the claim of family affection. The disciples of Jesus were caught between the demand for observance of the Sabbath and the need for food. Both claims may appear to represent certain aspects of the highest good. In an imperfect social order, and especially in times of rapid change, conflicts of obligation or of loyalties are likely to present themselves to individuals and to groups. Compromises may be necessary if adjustments are to be made to the new circumstances. They may be, in part, adaptations of the enlightened Christian conscience to new duties. Christian ethics, where there is a conflict, offers a presumption in favor of the welfare of the larger group.

Compromise under certain conditions may be the way to progress. Occasionally two persons or two groups find that their interests are opposed, or it may be merely that their views are different as to what is the proper course of action. So long as each stands solidly on his respective position and refuses to move, no solution is possible. Under such circumstances the road of progress is through compromise. Anyone who has served frequently on committees will recall that the report is sometimes not the complete wish of any one member, but a compromise which all of the members accept because it gives a tentative harmony which enables action to continue.

The very existence of orderly, peaceful, human relations or group life depends upon continuous compromise and adjustment to the ideas and convictions of others. In a society progressing in a normal way this interaction is of the very essence of life. We cannot withdraw from the world and live as hermits, nor live in a social vacuum. If we make decisions and attempt to carry them out in the actual world, some compromise may be necessary. All government is founded on compromise between different and sometimes conflicting groups. It proceeds by the process of give and take, by balancing opposing tendencies, and by a continuous process of adjusting rights and duties. Men give up some rights in order that they may enjoy others. The history of law is to a considerable extent a record of compromise between conflicting rights. The Federal Constitution of the United States, the state constitutions, as well as most of our laws are the result of compromise. Whether we interpret the Federal Constitution in terms of the adjustment between the individualistic tendencies and the demand for a more authoritative central power, or, as an economic document representing the division between the propertied and the non-propertied classes, we must recognize the result as a compromise. The very health of democracy is found in the willingness of divergent groups and individuals to discuss, to talk things out, to make compromises.

Through a little gain here and a little advantage there we move toward a better society.

There are various types of actions which under certain circumstances become essentially compromise. A few of these, from different areas of human relationships, need to be considered in more detail. In this way we shall see the nature and extent of the problems which face us all.

(1) Agreements. The duty as well as the value of keeping one's agreements as a sacred trust should be clear to everyone. For a person to be untrustworthy is to destroy a vital element of his personality. It is also a misuse of faith and confidence which tends to undermine social life. The welfare of both individuals and groups is at stake. For a nation to be untrustworthy is to cause a loss of respect both at home and abroad and to court disaster.

With these considerations in mind, there are those who claim that no compromise with our pledged word is ever justifiable. They shudder to think of linking such concepts as "Christian" and "compromise." Their position may be stated somewhat as follows: a mature morality does not go along with compromise. Our agreements are absolute obligations. If we permit exceptions it is difficult to tell where to stop. Before we realize what is happening, we are being influenced by expediency and self-interest. While it may appear easy to defend a certain exception on a certain occasion, it is impossible to get a principle that is satisfactory. Pious frauds and evasions soon become easy. Self-deceit, in the form of rationalization, is always lurking around the corner. There is also the fact that confidence tends to be impaired when exceptions are permitted. Persons may hesitate to make agreements with us, or to trust us, in the future. A man's integrity, a group's reputation, and honor are the things of greatest value.

Why shouldn't a man die if necessary to maintain his honor or the honor of his country? No compromise, they say, is to be tolerated.

On the other hand, there are many conscientious Christians, with whom I am inclined to agree, who think that in the concrete circumstances of life certain exceptions or compromises may actually forward the growth of the Kingdom of God. Not because they wish it, but due to the structure of the particular social situation, men face the alternative of sacrificing one value or another; and in some cases the selection of the greater value may mean the temporary denial or the change in application of our agreements. A man may be "honest" in a deal that is cruel and inhuman. He may obey the written code and lack the one thing which Jesus calls essential. Such questions cannot be solved apart from a consideration of the actual conditions in the midst of which men live.

When the problem is a choice between two conflicting duties, between two competing loyalties, or between one good and another good, the person who is morally and intellectually mature will weigh all the factors in the situation and decide according to his judgment of the relative values involved. In such a case, he is not denying the value of the lesser claim; he is merely choosing the lesser of two evils or the greater of two values, according to the way it is viewed. In making his choice he must take upon himself the consequences and the guilt, if any, for the violation of the value that has been sacrificed or compromised. There is a great difference between recognizing a particular exception to some standard and raising the exception into a new standard. Absolute rules fail to recognize the unique character of some life situations, and they fail to permit the creative adjustments of a person in a rapidly changing society.

Apparently there are conditions either explicit or implicit in all our pledges and agreements. Our ancestors usually added "D.V." (*Deo volente* or God Willing) to their agreements and contracts. They would do as specified unless some unforeseen event or circumstance, such as death, sickness, or accident interfered. Our courts are usually willing to nullify contracts made under the threat of force, or when fraud is present, or when unfair advantage is taken of some special knowledge or of the confidence of another. Contracts are sometimes annulled because changed social or economic conditions have made their terms unfair.

(2) Rules. Should rules once made be rigidly enforced or may exceptions be made? In order to have any orderly social life we need agreements, understandings, and rules. These may be deliberately formulated, or they may be ingrained in the habits of the persons and be largely unconscious. A person without any rules to guide him is likely to be one who acts capriciously. Some persons take the position that if a rule is good, it should be enforced in spite of any seeming injustice or any peculiarities of any particular case to which it is to be applied. To them it is more important that the rule shall be kept inviolate than that special circumstances shall be taken into account or an individual's rights considered. Many business executives, lawyers, teachers, moralists, and others set before themselves certain business, legal, educational, moral, or social rules which they accept as absolute in the sense that they are applied without exception or compromise. As particular problems arise, they find the solution not by examining the facts in the case, but by appeal to the absolute rule.

A fairly common practice in hospitals is to require the night nurses, before leaving in the morning, to see that patients are washed and ready for breakfast. In order to do so, patients must be wakened about five A.M., although breakfast is seldom served until two or more hours later. Imagine a patient who has found it difficult to sleep during the night, but who drops off to sleep toward morning, only to be wakened at five, and then left to lie awake for two hours until breakfast time. Yet, in one case, a protest only elicited the reply that this is a hospital rule and must be carried out accordingly. Granting for the moment that such a rule is a sane and logical one, are there not occasions when the breaking of the rule rather than its observance really carries out the purpose of the institution which is to help make people well?

A business executive told his secretary that, during a certain important board meeting, he was not to be interrupted, even for telephone calls. His secretary refused to call him when informed that his wife was involved in an automobile accident. Complications arose which probably could have been avoided had he been interrupted. The business executive, on learning of the facts later, reprimanded his secretary for her lack of discretion.

A business man once said to a subordinate, "Anybody can follow the rules. I pay you a good salary to know when to break them." The person who knows when rules should be followed and when they should be broken is a somewhat rare individual. Perhaps this is true because so many people find it difficult to distinguish between the essential and the accidental feature in a problem or situation. How easy it is to attempt to apply a good rule to a special situation when some unforeseen or accidental condition makes the rule inapplicable or even absurd. A proposition which is generally true may not be true, or not in the same way, when special circumstances are present. One of the common fallacies of human thinking is to believe and argue that what is true of a principle or a rule generally is also true of it under some special or accidental circumstances. Conversely, it is wrong to believe that what is true of a principle or rule under some special condition may be asserted of it, without further consideration, under any or all conditions. On the whole, it seems safe to say that a rule may be broken, and perhaps ought to be disregarded, when its breaking will greatly benefit some person and not harm anyone else.

One defense which is frequently made by the rigorist is: "If I make an exception for one person, then I shall have to make it for every one else." This, of course, is absurd. If some person comes along with equally good reasons for making an exception, then it should be made. To all other persons, if pressed for reasons, one can say: "Yes, I did make an exception for Mr. Blank, and if the conditions were the same in your situation I should do so for you. However, your case is quite different." This is not playing favorites or being partial. It is using one's intelligence. Such an approach is likely to elicit understanding and support from those for whom the rules were formulated. Obviously if too many exceptions have to be made, the rule is probably not a good one.

Rules tend to get out of date. Situations are likely to arise which no one imagined or took into account when the rules were drawn up. If applied rigidly they lead to an oppressive legalism and to irritation. Insistence upon hard and fast rules, which are to be applied without exception, may lead to certain evils. Those who enforce such rules may become satisfied with things-as-they-are and fall into a smug complacency. Those whom the rules affect may, after repeated irritations, be led to revolt against all rules and standards and develop a negative reaction. From then on full and hearty co-operation may be difficult if not impossible.

(3) Truthfulness. In the general principles of living the same problems arise as in the case of rules. For example,

practically all persons, the world over, recognize that truth-fulness is a virtue and that lying is a vice which tends to undermine wholesome human relationships. Does this mean then, as a few will maintain, that a man may not speak an untruth even to save the life of an innocent person who is being pursued by an infuriated mob?

Take the classical example of the Zurich theater manager who discovers one day that his theater is on fire backstage while a play is in progress. In some other incidents of that type the knowledge of the danger had led to a panic on the part of the audience and to serious injuries, even to a loss of life. The manager, therefore, goes before the audience and gives a false reason for discontinuing the performance. The audience leaves calmly and no injury results. Did the manager do right?

Doubtless we all know cases where the physicians and friends of some very sick person decide that the truth ought not to be told to the patient since it may militate against his recovery or lead him to give up the struggle against the disease. In such situations, the psychological factors may be crucial. May such exceptions or compromises with one's standard of truth-fulness be made?

In his book *Honesty,* Richard C. Cabot maintains that truthfulness or honesty is an absolute obligation and that exceptions are never justifiable under any circumstances. He thinks that if we permit exceptions it is difficult to get a principle which is satisfactory and that the area of lying tends to spread. Persons are also put on their guard, and confidence tends to be impaired.

On the other hand, probably a considerable majority of present-day students of morality agree that there are circum-stances when we need to make exceptions, even though they may involve the temporary denial of the obligation of truthfulness. Occasionally, in the concrete situations of life, men face the alternative of sacrificing one value or another. If a man feels that he should select one value rather than the other, he is not denying the worth of the value which for the time becomes subordinate. While the virtues and our everyday rules of conduct are good, there are occasions where exceptions must be made in the interest of some higher good. In such instances there is a great difference between recognizing an exception to our virtue, and raising this exception into a new standard or virtue. Virtues, rights, and duties, are instrumental and functional. They must serve life and not warp and stultify it.

Professor Hartmann [2] who supports the position of the liberal, rather than that of the rigorist or absolutist, points out that real moral life is not such that a man can always stand guiltless in it. In making his decision a man may have to take upon himself the consequences, and the guilt if any, for the violation of some value which he considers to be the lesser of the two involved. If he has weighed all the elements in the situation and makes his decision according to his best judgment of the values involved, he may emerge even stronger from such a conflict.

2. *Illustrations in Different Fields:*

In an article "Conscience and Circumstances," J. H. Marion, Jr., speaks about the Christian ideal of absolute racial equality. While accepting the principle as Christian he says that "many of us also know that in the South at least even the best of Christians cannot apply the principle absolutely without doing the cause of racial progress and justice harm." He gives the following illustration: "I think of a noble Quaker woman who came to the Carolinas a few years ago. Her husband was teaching in a university. At a meeting of our local interracial council one day she asked, somewhat heatedly, why she couldn't have Negroes in her home for meals or teas whenever she wanted them. Well, the Negroes themselves told her. Such an act would jeopardize not only her husband's position, they said, but also her personal Christian leadership in the community. It would inflame racial feeling against their own people and possibly bring to naught the patient forward steps of years. If their Quaker friend spurned their advice I never heard of it. Even if she has found a few cultured Negroes whom she invites to her table, it is safe to say that she does not do it as freely and as often as she may have done in the North. Her social morality in this field, in short, is definitely circumstantial." [3]

Most Christians will accept the ideal of co-operation and sharing in business and industrial relationships. Yet we know that business under our capitalistic order is not often operated in that way. Too frequently it is ruthless competition, *caveat emptor,* or "let the buyer beware," and the principle of every man for himself. While encouraging those who are working toward something better, we are forced to recognize and to compromise with the system as it is. We are forced to accept many things which we do not like because we wish to live.

Here is the case of an especially conscientious Christian fruit rancher in a Western state.[4] He is confronted with the following alternatives: "He can reduce the already insufficient wages of those who pick his crop, and thus make enough money to pay the interest on his loan at the bank. Or he can maintain wages and risk losing his heavily mortgaged ranch. Or, although he is an ardent Prohibitionist, he can sell the grape culls from his vineyard to be made into wine. By doing so he could possibly make enough extra money to maintain wages and pay his interest at the same time.

"Obviously, this man must compromise at some point. *The question is not whether to compromise but at what point to compromise.* Above all things he desires to be a loyal Christian. What then shall he do? Shall he go against his strong Christian convictions as a Prohibitionist and sell his grape culls? Shall he sacrifice his ranch in order to pay his workers better wages? Shall he decrease the pittance he is paying his workers in order to save his ranch from the bank, to preserve the integrity of his conscience about selling his grapes for wine, and to be in a position to employ workers another season?

"And now suddenly a new factor enters the situation. The workers join a newly organized union. The Christian rancher is confronted by a choice between quietly accepting the union and bargaining with it, and uniting with his fellow ranchers to fight it. If he accepts and bargains with the union he will gain the enmity of his fellow ranchers and the bank. If he fights the union he will incur the anger of the workers. How then can he remain loyal to the pure Christian faith and fellowship under any circumstances?"

Canon Peter Green tells of a young clergyman who was lunching on a Friday with his old Headmaster, also a clergyman. The younger clergyman, who was a particularly strict Anglo-Catholic, very particular about observing the fasts of the Prayer Book, ate heartily of the roast joint. When asked why he had done so, he replied: "Well, there was nothing the dear old fellow could have given me instead except bread and cheese, and if I had eaten only that he would have been vexed and unhappy. But it wasn't only that. You see, he's never thought anything about the fasts, and if I had insisted on keeping Friday it would have been setting myself up as better than he is. I may be a better Churchman. As a Christian I'm not fit to black his boots. So I just gobbled my beef with enjoyment." [5] Can we agree with Canon Green who suggests that in this case the young clergyman chose the more excellent way?

For years Christians have deplored the numerous divisions not only within the Christian church, but within particular denominational groups. Such divisions have affected the strength and the witness of the Christian church. Some lines used years ago by R. J. Campbell apply only to the most narrow and bigoted, but they represent an attitude which is too prevalent.

> We are God's chosen few.
> All others will be damned.
> There is no room in heaven for you,
> We can't have heaven crammed.

So long as religious groups maintain that they represent the truth and the right and refuse to compromise, there is no possibility of union or even of greater unity.

In recent years numerous problems have arisen in the field of politics and statesmanship. They have affected both our domestic and our international relations. For example, what was the State of Pennsylvania to do with the problem of bootleg coal? This problem became acute a few years ago. The coal operators appealed to the law. They took their stand on the rights of private property and the duty of the state to guard that property. They asked for armed intervention on the basis of their moral and legal rights. The unemployed miners, left stranded by the companies when they ceased to operate certain mines, asserted their right to live. They continued to dig the coal and to sell it. Governor Earle called it the "greatest conflict between moral and civil rights in Pennsylvania's history." He refused to call out the militia, but did agree to appoint a commission to study the problem.

During the last decade the Federal Government of the United States ceased its gold payments and started to regulate the currency. Was that act justified, or did it tend to "undermine the very foundation of morality," as some persons asserted? The opposition claimed that it was a repudiation of the government's contract to meet its obligations in gold, and that it changed the value of debts and altered contracts. Those who defended the government's policy pointed out that such action was justified on the basis of social welfare. Contracts were already being altered by changed economic conditions, including price fluctuations. The government, they said, was forced to take action to prevent grave injustices and possibly economic collapse.

How about the action of Mr. Chamberlain at Munich in 1939? He was bitterly condemned as a betrayer of Czechoslovakia. He was also praised for his efforts in behalf of the peace of Europe. Did he do right in seeking some compromise which he thought might avoid a general war? Clearly the situation at that time was complicated. If Mr. Chamberlain acted on the basis of national self-interest alone, or if he was willing to have peace only because it was a little nation which paid the price, his action was to be condemned. If he weighed all the factors involved and chose what he considered to be the greater value under the circumstances, he should not be condemned morally, even though many persons may now feel, in the light of later events, that he chose unwisely.

In international relations the ways of adjustment and compromise may be necessary if conflicts and wars are to be avoided. So long as nations insist upon their supposed "rights of absolute sovereignty" and refuse to consider any interests except their own, there is little hope for international peace or good will. Many persons supported such organizations as the League of Nations and the World Court because those institutions offered avenues for mutual understanding and hence for compromise and conciliation.

3. *Some Conclusions Regarding Compromise*

Now that we have considered various types of compromise and have illustrated some of the problems involved, we are ready to draw a few generalizations. First, there are some types of compromise that are clearly immoral. These include the indulgence of some personal inclination or desire, attempts to "split the difference" between a line of duty and some vice, or other actions which are the result of moral laxity or coward-ice.

Second, compromise, under some circumstances, may be the way to progress, and higher values. Some of the examples we have given from various walks of life seem to make this clear. Compromise may indicate a willingness to make adjust-ments so that normal social relations can continue. Such compromises may actually forward the step by step growth toward the Kingdom of God.

Third, as individuals and as groups, the important thing for us is to keep moving in the right direction. By no means should we lower our goals or our ideals. They should be held clearly and tenaciously as guides to action. Ideals have been compared to the stars above us; we do not reach them, but like the sailors on the high seas, we get our direction from them. However, to compare our ideals with the stars is not very accurate. Some of our ideals we should actually reach, others tend to grow and to expand as we move in their direc-tion. While we hold our ideals before us, we also need to keep in contact with the actualities of our present life situations. This will enable us to select our next steps and to make such immediate practical decisions as will forward our cause. We shall see what can be done to make the actual situation somewhat better. Any compromise will be for the sake of lifting men to a higher level of living. A man needs an intelligent philosophy of compromise so that action will not be paralyzed, and so that he will not become disloyal or hypocritical in the presence of his ideals.

Fourth, the stand which a man should take cannot be determined by rules in advance. Occasionally two or more intelligent, conscientious, and mature persons, after weighing the relevant factors in connection with some problem, will decide differently. This may frequently occur when the two sides are fairly evenly balanced. The essence of a mature morality is the ability and the willingness to weigh all the relevant factors and to make one's decision on the basis of the values involved.

When a man faces a law, or custom, or some social code, which he believes to be wrong or immoral but which is accepted and supported by a majority of his fellowmen, what is he to do? There are a number of possible lines of action. He may say, first, that while he does not believe the judgment of the majority to be wise or just, since he believes in the democratic method and wishes to be a good citizen, he will accept the decision and co-operate in carrying it out. Second, he may conform to the requirements while making clear his position and agitating for revision. Third, he may refuse to give in or to compromise if he considers the issue of supreme importance. In this case, he should make his position clear, refuse to obey the law or custom or code, and be ready to meet the consequences or to face the penalty without flinching. This is the stand of the martyr. If the latter stand is reasonable and in line with an emerging justice, other men will probably come to see its rightness and give it support. The martyr may be stoned one year and praised the next—or, should I say, by the next generation.

The man who is true to his convictions is admired. But not so the fanatic who often wrecks good causes by refusing wise concessions, by making no allowances for circumstances, and by recognizing no qualifying principles. The fanatic is one who is unable to entertain more than one idea at a time. He is legalistic and intolerant. Goodness is positive and personal, rather than negative and formal. The Pharisees of Jesus' day were not "bad" people. They were legalistic and rigoristic. They thought that because a law was "good" in one circumstance, it was "good" under any and all conditions. Jesus was sometimes more disturbed by the wooden goodness of the respectable people of his day than by the badness of the less respectable members of society. Paul spoke of making himself "all things to all men." To the Jew he became as a Jew, and to those without the Law as without the Law. To build a better society men have to ask, "What is the next possible step?" The old must continue until it can be replaced by the new.

When a problem of right and wrong confronts him, the morally mature man will examine and carefully consider all the factors involved in the selection of each of the possible lines of action. In the light of his comparison of the values involved, he will make his decision. Morality is not a rigid set of rules. It includes growth and devotion to an ideal. Christian morality includes love for God and for man. Loyalty to Christ means loyalty to the best possible life in the situation in which a man finds himself. Perhaps that is the only thing on which he should be unwilling to compromise.

Experimentation

If right and wrong are not something absolute and fixed, so that circumstances in life can be disregarded, how are men to discover what to do? We live in a world where there are right and wrong ways of doing things in every area of human relationships and in a world where we must make decisions continuously. Tradition and habit make it easy for us to hold on to the familiar ways of doing things. Social pressure makes it difficult for us to refuse to follow the crowd. Some persons avoid doubts of conventional beliefs and actions by closing their minds to all contradictory evidence, or by an appeal to some authority to support their own views. In the field of morality, the authoritarian has been fairly completely in control in the past, and this is in large part responsible for the fact that moral codes and ideals have been in disrepute. It also explains why the advice of so-called moral leaders is so frequently ignored, and why so many have lost faith in all standards and even in life itself. Authoritarian ethics are likely to be negative in attitude, to delay progress in a rapidly changing society, and to be destructive of moral perspective since acts are condemned regardless of whether or not they are fundamental to wholesome living.

In an earlier chapter we pointed out that the role of authority has been growing weaker and weaker in Western civilization, except in certain totalitarian states. This is due in part to influences that have come down to us from the Renaissance and the Reformation, but more particularly to the development of scientific method, to theories of evolution and relativity, and to the growth of the democratic spirit which emphasizes the worth of the individual and his right to think and to judge for himself. The rapid changes in our mode of living and working, and the growth of historical criticism which has been applied to the development of religion and morality have also been significant. The prevalent attitude is not "as it was in the beginning is now and ever shall be," but "to prove all things" and to hold fast only to that which stands the test.

Modern men are not averse to authority as such. In fact, they are eager for light and for guidance which is based upon expert and upon experimental evidence. In this sense any morality which will appeal to them must be authoritative. Much of our knowledge, in all fields, comes from the past and from the testimony of our fellows. Authority or testimony that is open to free and honest study and to critical evaluation is a legitimate source of knowledge. Where authorities are supported by evidence, men often prefer to go to the evidence. Where the authorities make unsupported pronouncements they feel that such claims ought to be open to question and investigation. When authorities are external and arbitrary, men are likely to fight back at them in rebellion.

The great discoveries of recent centuries have come when men have freed their minds from fixed authorities and have applied their intelligence to the facts of life and of human experience. Is this attitude and experimental method applicable to the field of morals? We have seen that both morality in general and Christian morality are the result of long periods of development in the course of which new elements were assimilated. The Biblical record shows a remarkable and continuous development from early primitive ideals and practices to the lofty heights of ethical idealism set forth in the New Testament. Christian ethics has never been a closed or static system. Apparently there has been much experimentation, even though it has often been only partly conscious and ill directed. Is modern man able to do consciously and more intelligently what has been going on through the slow and painful process of unconscious adjustment and conflict?

Since we live in a social order which is undergoing rapid changes, and which, in addition, is a mixture of good, evil, and neutral elements, an increasing number of the leaders of our moral and spiritual life feel that experimentation is not only possible but essential. Practices which originated in an agricultural or a feudal society are intermingled with conduct and laws which are applicable only to a complex industrial society. The strains and tensions, as well as the open conflicts, of our age indicate that codes and ways of living must be adapted to the needs of life today. Changes in our society ought to be gradual and intelligent rather than occasional and violent. The problems of adjustment are continuous and call for a mature and reflective morality.

In a book entitled *Write Your Own Ten Commandments,*[6] Bernard E. Meland, who is thinking more largely in terms of one's personal code, asks, "Why should everyone try to achieve moral excellence in exactly the same way?" While there are "certain broad, basic patterns of human living" that lead the way to effectiveness for all normal persons, the diversity of traits and talents makes it essential that we work out specific codes for ourselves. We should first engage in self-examination to discover the pattern of our living. For some persons an act is approved or disapproved because it is "moral or immoral"; for others "good taste" and artistry will be important; for others it is a matter of "mental and social hygiene"; for still others conduct is motivated by practical considerations relating to the institutional life. Since the chief end of man is to grow, each man ought to find significance in developing the distinctive capacities which he possesses. Dr. Meland sets forth some good suggestions as to what might be included in a modern man's ten commandments when they are worked out experimentally.

In *The Moral Crisis in Christianity,*[7] Justin Wroe Nixon has pointed out that where men are dealing with their problems simply on the basis of the uncritical acceptance of tradition, we find the attitudes of confusion and pessimism, but that wherever men are intelligently experimenting in an attempt to discover better ways, there we find hope and confidence. Ralph W. Sockman in *Morals of Tomorrow*[8] says that it is impossible for "one generation to fix final codes of ethics for the next." Moral principles must be tested out in new situations. Only those who lack faith in man's creative effort and in "a living Creative Spirit" demand finality in the field of morals. He says that the whole system of ethics seems to be open for investigation.

The late Canon B. H. Streeter has pointed out in *Moral Adventure*[9] not only the need for experimentation in the field of morality, but certain principles that must be followed if men are to profit by experimentation. I am indebted to him and to the others whom we have mentioned for suggestions regarding some of these principles. To profit by experimentation in the realm of morals there are four principles which need to be kept clearly before us.

First, experiments must be arranged and directed by persons who have as complete knowledge and experience as possible in the field in which the experiment is to be made. The person who is to experiment needs to know what has been done before in the field, that is, he needs to know the past and what experiments have already been made. He also needs to know the present facts and circumstances. To repeat experiments which have proven destructive, in the experience of the race, or to explore again all the blind alleys of the past, would be folly indeed. Men do not have to steal in order to discover the effect of stealing. They do not need to contract all the ugly diseases in order to know that it is wise to avoid them. In the field of diet men need to accept some experience and authority from the past, or they may not be around to carry on more valuable experiments. In this connection Christianity supplies the experimenter with a vast amount of rich moral experience. This includes the codes of conduct, the accounts of the lives of numerous persons, and the long-time trends found in Biblical literature. While some of the codes and the behavior patterns have been outgrown, there are others that represent mature insights into the conditions of all high living. Such a background is needed if one is to have both historical and moral perspective. In morals, no more than in mathematics, can the individual clear the field and start out for himself as if nothing had been done before.

Second, no one should attempt to test any new proposals, or to carry out experimentation, unless, on the basis of all the available evidence, the probability of success appears to be great. When we are dealing with persons we need to be even more cautious than when we are dealing with non-human materials. Much of the apparatus of the physics or chemistry laboratory can be easily replaced, but not so the disturbed human emotions, the distorted conduct, or the life of a person. This ought not, however, to turn us from all experimentation. When emotions and conduct are warped or distorted, and when lives are imperilled or broken by some present method of acting or by an existing system, then men ought to seek to discover better ways, even though there are risks involved. No area of life is so sacred that we ought to refuse to attempt to improve it, especially if unsatisfactory results are in evidence.

Third, an experiment in the field of morality ought to be carried out only when there is a clear conviction that it will increase human welfare. To experiment or to break a code of conduct merely to gratify personal desire or convenience is clearly immoral. This should not blind us, however, to the legitimate use of experimentation. To depart from some custom, or law, or previous practice because we think that it is productive of evil, and that some new path will lead toward more satisfactory results, is justified. Mature men will ever be conscious of the need to experiment upward rather than downward. They will, in the words of Jesus, desire "to fulfill" and "not to destroy" the moral law. Jesus' attitude toward life encouraged the spirit of seeking or of quest for the better way. Progress in morality comes through improving or in outdoing what has been done before.

Fourth, experiments, in the field of morality, like experiments in other fields, always go on within a frame of reference, a point of view, or a structure which rests upon a foundation of faith. Just as there are various assumptions and postulates in science, like the uniformity of natural law, which are accepted even though they cannot be proven beyond a doubt, so in Christian ethics there are certain basic attitudes toward life that are accepted because they have been found to be valuable and to make life worthwhile. That life is worth living, and that there is meaning in the universe, are postulates of faith for which there is much evidence, even though we may not be able to convince the skeptic who finds it hard to believe. In the field of human relationships certain things will be found to be true only if men believe them to be true, and will live and sacrifice on their behalf. If men believe that the world can be made better, they are likely to live in a better world than they would have lived in otherwise. On the basis of their beliefs or convictions men enter into certain contracts, agreements, or life commitments. These commitments are of great importance, and they ought not to be forgotten. They should be made only after we have examined or weighed the facts and have reached clear convictions. But after we have made these decisions, our energy should be directed toward the success of our chosen venture or ideal. To remain in a detached and critical attitude may mean failure. In making experiments we need to keep in mind these life commitments. This is especially true of the bonds of matrimony since the deepest and richest experiences arise only when there is complete trust and confidence. This is the danger and mistake of trial marriages, since one or both persons may sit back critically and make no active effort to produce the success which may be possible.

Fruitful experimentation will nearly always be on the margin of an existing body of experience. It is likely to be in the nature of adaptations and adjustments to existing codes and practices. Today, as in the past, there needs to be a gradual displacement of less adequate by more adequate ways of living.

CHAPTER VI

RELIGION, ETHICAL AND UNETHICAL

AMONG THE CAUSES of the present confusion of standards we included a loss of religious passion and a separation of religion from morality and from everyday life. We also suggested that religion may have undergone some disintegration with a resulting loss of prestige and power. Such a thing has happened at various times in the past. There have been periods of decline as well as periods of renaissance or reformation. If Christians view the tasks of men as part of man's duty to God, then the relation between morality and religion is exceedingly important. If we are to look to religion for help, we shall need to ask, "To what kind of religion?"

Religion is under attack in the modern world as it has not been for centuries. There is a growing revolt which has expressed itself in indifference among some groups and in open revolt among other groups. This is especially true in some parts of the world. For example, in Russia, religion and the churches have been attacked and religious leaders have been persecuted. There have been "no God" exhibits and antireligious campaigns. While religion has not been eliminated, the churches have been stripped of all their functions and privileges except worship. The leaders of the Communist movement felt that in order to build a better society they needed to get rid of religion, since religion centered men's attention upon another world and retarded progress in the present world. It was, they said, "the opiate for the people." They felt that if they limited religious activities to worship then religion would become impotent and harmless. In Germany, some of the leaders, like Niemöller, who have refused to submit to Nazi control, have been sent to concentration camps. While religion has not been banned in the fascist countries, there has been an attempt to bring it under control, and some would say to eliminate many of the things which are most distinctly "Christian." Some of the leaders of the Nazi movement have asserted that they are creating a new Teutonic or German morality that will rank higher than Christian morality. In Mexico and in Turkey there has been opposition to the churches. In Japan, many of the Christian missionaries have had to leave, even before the outbreak of war.

A considerable part of the opposition to religion arises from the type of religion which existed in the countries mentioned. For example, in Mexico, the great cathedrals were surrounded by the wretched hovels of the masses. There was little attempt, if any, to make an application of the principles of religion to the problems of the day. One student of Mexico, unfortunately, felt obliged to say that an atheistic government had done more for the people in ten years than was done for them under four hundred years of church control. While this is a questionable statement, it contains considerable truth so far as social welfare measures are concerned. In fascist countries part of the opposition is due to the fact that the fascist philosophy is in such sharp conflict with the Christian interpretation of life.

Today there is tension between church and state in many parts of the world, and many powerful movements are definitely anti-religious. This rightly disturbs those who are interested in religion, and leads them to ask why this should be so. The one good thing that may come from such hostility is that religion may come to mean something more definite against a background of opposition. It may bring into sharper relief the things for which the Christian church stands. Persons who were merely nominal Christians may leave the church. Christianity has had its greatest growth during the periods of opposition.

There is another type of revolt that may be more accurately called indifference. One of the main examples of this is the increasing lack of contact and sympathy between the church and labor in the United States. In England, laboring groups are quite sympathetic to the church and many labor leaders are within the churches and give them active support. Much support for the labor movement also comes from the churches. On the continent of Europe, labor, on the whole, has been antagonistic to the church and has supported anti-clerical movements. In America there has been a tendency for labor and the church to go their own separate ways. Indifference, rather than either active support or active opposition, has been the rule, at least in the larger centers. That should cause us concern, since labor is an increasing group, and since we are becoming a highly industrialized nation. At least in our cities, there has been a tendency for the Protestant Church to be definitely middle class. There are very few labor churches or churches that are located in thickly populated labor districts. President Coffin of Union Theological Seminary has said that there is a danger that we shall have a class church and a church-less class.[1] This is exceedingly unfortunate, both for labor and for the church.

Unethical Religion

Why are persons and groups criticizing and even rebelling against the church? Is it possible that they are revolting against what is not really religion? The church has often raised symbols to remind it of its object of devotion; then, in some cases, it has worshipped the symbols and forgotten its object of devotion. The church has built great organizations to help carry out its task in the world, but in some instances, it has forgotten the task and has centered attention on the institution as an end in itself. The church has developed an elaborate theology, but sometimes some of its doctrines offend the modern conscience or sense of what is right and wrong. In these and other ways it has lost power and appeal or has even become corrupt. Unethical religion is one of the greatest foes of genuine religion. In this section we shall consider five ways in which religion may lose its ethical drive or its power to move men and to transform the world.

First, *through a growing secularism*. This may be due to the fact that secular life is encroaching on the church, or it may be because the church is lowering its ideals and thus tending to reflect its environment. We do know that the church is being pushed out of more and more areas of life. Once the church set the standard and ideals for all of life. Higher education was the child of the church, but today even most of the schools and universities which were started by the churches have been separated from church control. Art was once definitely religious in motivation. Today it is "Art for art's sake." Philosophy, during the Middle Ages, was an ally of the church. The separation started during the Renaissance and proceeded rapidly during "The Enlightenment" of the eighteenth century and before long many philosophers, looking more to natural science, developed an anti-religious bias. Science not only naturalized the world but reduced man to the terms of a mechanical behaviorism. Business men say that "business is business" and ask the churches not to meddle in business affairs or to criticize its standards. Even marriage, once under the exclusive jurisdiction of the churches, is no longer so.

The churches, from another point of view, are tending to reflect their environments instead of transforming those environments. They are not making clear the things for which they stand in the modern world. Too often religion is made to support the doctrines and practices of an acquisitive society. When this happens modern culture suffers from lack of goals and a sense of direction. History seems to show that when the church ceases to transform society, it tends to become conformed to it.

After pointing out how secularism causes life to fall apart and lose its sense of wholeness, by pursuing each interest and activity as an end in itself, William Clayton Bower says: "It may be well to remind ourselves that religion is as much subject to the same process of secularization as the other phases of human life. When religion ceases to be the organizing center of the operative values in every dimension of the common life, it, too, becomes just another specialized interest, preoccupied with its institutions, its theology, its ritual, and its tradition. It then becomes another factor of personal and social disintegration, having lost its sensitivity to moral and social issues and having become as destructive of human and spiritual values as are exploitative economics or politics. . . . A secularized religion whose primary concern is with tradition, metaphysical theological formulas, and antiquated ceremonial has no contribution to make to an education for a new world-order. Such a religion can only hamper and embarrass it. The only religion that can contribute to the building of a new world-order through education is a religion functionally related to the experience of growing persons as they face the living issues of a real and present world in terms of dynamic and growing spiritual values." [2]

Second, religion may lose its ethical drive through *sectarianism, institutionalism,* and *tribalism.* While there are differences between these terms, they are also similar and may be considered in the same section. The numerous divisions have hurt the church, especially in so far as these divisions have fostered the spirit of sectarianism. Carlyle likened sectarianism to the man who mistook the umbrella over his head for the whole sky's broad canopy. It sees only one point of view and is intolerant toward those who differ from that point of view. It is to blame for the fact that we do not have a closer union in many efforts which are being put forward for a better world. It explains the overcrowding of churches in some areas and the lack of churches in other places. The spirit of sectarianism offends many persons and keeps them outside the churches.

Institutionalism may accompany and reinforce sectarianism. Institutions of many kinds are essential in any society. An institution consists of an idea, an interest, or a purpose with an organization or structure to carry the idea into action. The great institutions are the forms which human thought and energy take when they are directed over a period of time to some particular subject. They profoundly affect the attitudes and habits of persons as they grow up in them, and thus they are important in moral training. The child's code tends to develop in harmony with the standards and practices of his group. Institutions, however, tend to harden and crystallize in definite forms around which cluster sentiments, customs, and beliefs. When they become rigid, they tend to suppress, rather than to express, the free creative spirit of man. So it is that an institution or organization which is established to carry out some mission may come later on to be regarded as an end in itself, instead of as a means to some great end. This is institutionalism. When churches stop attempting to change society for the better they tend to sanction the *status quo*, to become opponents of all change, and to lose their drive and power.

Tribalism is another form of this same danger. It may accompany or be reinforced by sectarianism and institutionalism. Appeal is made to one segment or section or group in society. There may be an attempt to organize society on the basis of a social or economic class, a racial group, or along state or national lines. Religion may be used as a sanction for these distinctions. In the United States, the churches North and South have tended to follow, rather than to transcend, sectional, class, and racial lines. When they do so, they tend to betray both man and God. May I give two illustrations.

"The Friendly Visitor had been asked to call on a young Russian Jewish woman who had not been long in this country. She found the young woman homesick, lonely and despondent in spite of her new and shining American home. The husband, an ambitious American Jew, had evidently done his best to encourage the Americanization of his wife by taking an apartment in a section of the city settled largely by the older immigration, but the newcomers had been conspicuously ignored by their Gentile neighbors, and the young wife felt bitterly alone. The Friendly Visitor was welcomed with almost pathetic appreciation as the young woman was soon to become a mother and was fearful of the experience amid alien and unaccustomed surroundings. On leaving, the visitor, who had offered to make necessary arrangements with doctor and district nurse, said cheerfully, 'Now if you are alone and need me quickly just call one of your neighbors and she can telephone me.' The shadow of despondency again settled on the face of the young woman as she answered, 'There isn't anyone to call. All the people who live around here are Christians.' "[3]

An outstanding Negro preacher, one of the most brilliant of the younger men, tells about being asked to preach in a leading white church in a Western American city. He preached in the morning and was well received. Many complimentary remarks were heard concerning the way he conducted the service. Wishing to remain in the city until Monday, he decided to return to the church in the evening to hear the local minister. He took a seat near the rear on the main floor. Immediately he noticed some commotion among the ushers and a hurried conference. Then one of the ushers came and asked him if he would mind going into the rear of the gallery.

Sectarianism, institutionalism, and tribalism, separately or in combination, make it especially difficult for men to learn the larger meaning of loyalty. The religion of Jesus was not tribal; it was universal. It transcended the distinctions of color, race, and class. Our divided world is in desperate need of a greater degree of unity. Can the church, in its present divided state, appeal with consistency for unity and harmony in the nation and in the world?

Third, religions lose their power and ethical drive when they become *means of escape from the world*. One means of escape is to retreat from the problems of this world into otherworldliness. It has expressed itself in asceticism and monasticism. Men may withdraw from the world and live as hermits while attempting to deny or to crush the interests of earthly life. They may gather together in orders or societies spending much time in contemplation, prayer, and religious rites, while denying themselves the pleasures of ordinary life. During some periods in history the monasteries have performed a real service in keeping religion alive. There have been times when escape to the catacombs was the only means of survival. However, when such an attitude leads persons to put up with misery and need here and now because of the hope of a better life in the next world it may become vicious. The message of "good news" which Jesus brought proclaimed liberty and life for the physically maimed and sick, for the socially outcast, and for those who were morally and spiritually disinherited. He was realistic in dealing with the contemporary issues of his day and he did not encourage otherworldliness.

Today there are two influences that tend to keep religion from coming into close and vital contact with the present world. They are operating from entirely different backgrounds and with quite different purposes. The first includes those movements like Communism which have been unfriendly to religion and wish to see it vanish. We have already spoken of the opposition to religion in Russia and the attempt to reduce the functions of the church to worship. After the Revolution in Russia in 1918 some of the Protestant churches began to grow and to concern themselves with the total life of the people. The Communist leaders were fearful of the influence of the churches and forbade them from taking part in social reconstruction. They were forced to become merely worshipping bodies. Those who are tempted to criticize the Communists too severely will do well to remember that American capitalist society has demanded much the same thing of the churches—that they "preach religion" and leave political, economic, and social problems alone. When religious institutions have been controlled by wealthy groups with special privileges in society, religion sometimes has really been "an opiate for the people."

Another influence that tends in the same direction is Neo-Supernaturalism, the Barthian movement, or the Crisis Theology. Karl Barth, Emil Brunner, and others have been leaders of the movement. God, we are old, is so far beyond man and every human interest that he must be characterized as "wholly other." God is not found in history nor in nature. He is even beyond man's thinking. He is not discovered by anything we can do, nor can we do anything to change the world order. All that man can do is to stand in awe before

God's majesty and power. God breaks in, so to speak, through the crisis. Man merely submits.

We are witnessing today the rise of numerous religious sects which are emotional, individualistic, and apocalyptic in their outlook. They put the emphasis on eccentric forms of religious expression, like speaking with tongues, falling and jerking, and lapses into unconsciousness. These movements may be for their members, who tend to come from the low income groups, means of escape from a world that has neglected them.

The tendency of the Neo-Supernaturalists and of the religious sects, about which we have just spoken, is to direct attention to another world almost exclusively. The problems of this world are not important. When religion becomes so completely concerned with the supernatural world and permits itself to disregard, or to be used to sanction injustices in this world, it will be scorned and rejected by large numbers of people.

Another means of escape may be in the form of aesthetic and ritualistic religion. Beauty and ritual may be splendid helps in religious worship. If they help men to feel the presence of God, and if they stimulate them to holier living and greater deeds, they are of real worth. What I wish to say is that they ought not to be ends in themselves. If they keep people content with an unjust society and occupy complete attention, they may be forms of escape.

Fourth, religion may lose its ethical drive through *a separation of the religious and the practical life*. This might be a form of escape. However, I am thinking here of the separation which does not include escape into another world. One form of this separation is to be found when religion is largely verbal. It consists of generalities and platitudes. There is the language of religion but little more. In the same way a "verbal morality" may continue after the actuality, which it once symbolized, has withered away. Some religion might be likened to an orchestra in which the members spent all their time eulogizing their leader and never played any great music. It may consist in platitudes or it may be a nominal religion which arises in tradition and continues through custom. The story is told of a man who was working on a building one day. Something went wrong and he swore a little. A deacon who was passing by at the time remonstrated with him. The man replied: "Look here, deacon, you pray a bit; I swear a bit. Neither one of us means anything by it. What is the difference?" It is possible that one might even be nearer to God in seeking what is in line with his purpose while denying God's existence, than he would be in supporting injustices while praising his name.

The separation may arise through external pressure. When ministers touch life in certain vital spots, they are sometimes told to "preach religion." The following quotation speaks for itself:

"The duty of a minister is to preach the spiritual life. But he must confine himself to preaching the ideals, not to preaching on practical method for realizing those ideals.

"Ministers of religion make a mistake if they turn their thoughts and their words from man's soul to considerations of his bread and butter, his cake, his pie, his clothes, his wages, his working hours. These considerations are ephemeral whereas the soul of man is a subject beyond time." [4]

The use made of the principle of vicarious sacrifice affords a good illustration of the separation about which we have been talking. The principle of vicarious sacrifice runs through human life from ancient to modern times. There is a reality of vicarious sacrifice in the death of Jesus Christ on the cross. It revealed the principle of life at the heart of the universe.

But what do Christians often do? Instead of asking men and women to live according to the sacrificial ideal, many persons emphasize the sacrifice of one innocent person in our place and say that, in this way, God is pleased. All we have to do is to accept this deed for ourselves, as if it were to happen at one time and in one place only. Yet the real religion of Jesus is sacrificial in a much more vital sense and calls on all men to live lives of sacrifice.

A few years ago the newspapers carried a story of an incident that took place at the hearings before the United States Senate committee on the wages and hours bill. A prominent textile manufacturer, it was said, shocked both the Republican and the Democratic members of the committee by telling them that he thought eleven dollars a week was a fair and reasonable minimum wage. He also said that he had "allowed" a number of grandmothers to work for six dollars a week during the depression "as a humane thing." When questioned, he is said to have replied, "Why, I've never thought of paying men on the basis of what they need. I don't inquire into what they want. I pay men for efficiency." Then he went on to say that "Those other things, social welfare stuff," have to do with the emotional side of living. He attended to them, he said, in his church connections. The papers also added that he opens his factory every day with prayer. The men who pray on Sunday and then "prey on their neighbors" the other six days of the week are the ones who bring religion into disrepute. When religion degenerates, it is especially distastrous. As Shakespeare puts it:

> For sweetest things turn sourest by their deeds;
> Lilies that fester smell far worse than weeds.

The outstanding preacher of an ethical religion, Dr. Harry Emerson Fosdick, after quoting these lines from Shakespeare, says: "So an unintelligent and unethical religion has held up social progress, blessed social abominations like slavery and war, preached soft contentment with shameful present conditions in hope of a future heaven, or satisfied itself with relieving distresses caused by an inhuman social order without changing the social order itself." [5]

When ethics and religion disintegrate or when they are separated there is a damage to both. Morality tends to lack drive while religion tends to become immoral and to lose much of its significance. There is a further tendency for the relations between men to be governed by self-interest and force.

One of the dangers in the modern world is that the great mass of fairly respectable or "good" people lack the insight and the ethical purpose to move out of their familiar ruts and do the things that need to be done. In speaking about "The Evil that Good People Do," Dr. Harry A. Overstreet says that "When millions of honest people are dead set against doing things in the ways they now need to be done, something is bound to crack. Today the world is cracking all around us. Only incidentally is this happening because there are villains on the loose. Basically it is happening because millions of us 'good people' have not yet learned to be good enough. Our spirits are willing, but our minds are muddled. . . . It is the good people—not the conspicuously bad—who invariably do most damage. For good people are legion. They set the pace and establish the tone of a society. Their intentions are excellent; but when their minds are geared to wrong ideas, they have a way of going forth in all innocence and earnestly doing the things that precisely ought not to be done." [6]

"One would have a difficult time," says a Professor of Ethics and Philosophy of Religion in one of our theological seminaries, "with a thesis to the effect that rank and file

Christians show a superior sense of moral values in their philosophy of life. Rare exceptions, of course, illuminate the highroad across the centuries. . . . It is simply untrue that a sincere profession of Christian faith guarantees quality in moral understanding. Opportunities considered, Christians are deplorable in moral illiteracy. Like the good people about whom Jesus spoke, religion ofttimes sanctifies their prejudices until they are actually made worse by it. . . . After piling the evidence mountain-high, Kirby Page once wrote: 'It is a dangerous delusion to assume that a person who makes a sincere confession of faith in Christ will hereafter lead an ethical life.' " [7]

Fifth, religion may become unethical because of a *separation of theological and ethical ideals*. Morality does not imply any specific set of theological and religious beliefs, but the presence of religious beliefs or rites that are out of harmony with mature moral standards or ideals may do much harm to the growth of religion and the respect with which it is regarded. When moral standards advance very far beyond the standards implied by the prevailing religious outlook, religious leaders will be forced to do one of two things. They may restate their religious beliefs and bring them into harmony with the current moral ideas. This is sometimes spoken of as "the moralization of theology." If they do not do this, they may reject the moral ideals and appeal to tradition or to some supernatural sanction. If men are to interpret their duties as "duties to God," then God and religion must be interpreted in harmony with an enlightened moral consciousness.

In order to see this problem most clearly it would be necessary to go back to primitive times and to trace the development of morality in relation to religion. The early Hebrews, for example, made remarkable progress in continuously adding moral content to their religion. The Old Testament is in part an account of a gradual ascent from primitive ideas and practices to the high level of the teachings of Jesus in the Sermon on the Mount. Readers familiar with the Old Testament will know that it does not present one moral level throughout its pages. The development of morality is represented by the changing attitudes toward slaves, foreigners, women, and also toward God. There is a growing insight into the worth of human personality and a growing appreciation of the moral foundations of personal and social life. Some of the earlier codes sanction the selling to an alien of the flesh of an animal that had died of itself (Deuteronomy 14:21), whereas, in the New Testament, the forgiveness of enemies, even those who are foreigners, is taught. In the early manuscripts, God is represented as a local deity who is interested in the military exploits of his people. He gives directions for the slaughter of the Amalekites, men, women, and children, and encourages blood revenge. In the later portions of the Old Testament and in the New Testament, the idea of God is spiritual and ethical. God is interested in purity and righteousness. He is a loving father who does not desire that "one of these little ones shall perish." The moral ideals attributed to God are a good indication of the moral level or maturity of a people.

Religion may be an aid to a growing morality, or it may be a retarding force. The great Hebrew prophets were continually bringing under moral condemnation the organized religion of their times because it failed to meet the needs of men. Later, Jesus of Nazareth carried on this task of challenging and enlightening the consciences of men. He found some publicans and "sinners" more willing to respond than were some of the respected religious leaders of his day. We have already spoken about the Protestant Reformation and interpreted it as in part a trend toward the personal and the ethical. Martin

Luther and other leaders protested against doctrines and practices which they considered immoral.

While we admire and respect the leaders of the Reformation,
they have not relieved us of burdens of a similar nature. In
the first place, Protestantism was born in prescientific days
when very few of the dominant ideas which constitute the
background of modern thinking were in existence. The Reformation confessions and creeds were formulated before men
were thinking in terms of the inductive method, the Coper-
nican astronomy, the Newtonian physics, the theory of evolution, or the theory of relativity, to mention just a few
conceptions. In the second place, the principles of the Reformation themselves were not carried out to their logical
conclusions. Before many years, a new legalism and a new
authoritarianism were beginning to stifle men's thinking and
to retard their creative moral ideals. The moralization of
theology must continue.

A study of the history of Christian thought will indicate that
doctrines of God, of salvation, and of sin and punishment have
changed from age to age. These changes have been a response
to the new knowledge and the "intellectual climate" of the day
including the developing moral ideals of men. Changes in the
social and political organization of society tend to lead men
to revise or restate their religious conceptions. Anselm could
interpret God and salvation in terms of a feudal society. Such
conceptions would not be likely to win men today. Our age
has the same right, as past ages, to state its deepest convictions in meaningful concepts. Yet many churches are still
burdened with theological doctrines that offend the moral
sense of educated people.

Man tends to transfer to a higher power, called God, those
qualities which he feels are permanent and of real worth. He
feels that the characteristics and ideals toward which he is

pressing are already present and fulfilled in God. While God, the reality, may be the same "yesterday and today," the ideas which men hold concerning God do change from time to time. The character which man has attributed to God has always tended to represent the highest moral standard of the age. However, as man develops to higher stages of morality, many of his earlier conceptions of the deity will satisfy him no longer, and consequently they must be revised to meet his more advanced moral ideals. With the deepening of man's moral insight and the widening of his intellect, there will be an ever-enlarging conception of God. Any act or attribute which would be considered immoral if done by man must not be attributed to God. For this reason men cannot now accept many deeds and sayings which have been attributed to God in the past. This is true whether these sayings and deeds appear in the Biblical literature or in an older theology.

If men are to worship God today, He must above all be represented as a Moral Being. Christians worship an "eternal goodness," a God of the highest moral integrity. The Christian believes that there is a moral demand for belief in God and that this conception finds its richest meaning in the moral realm. As a result of this we cannot accept many of the views of God which have been set forth in the past. A God who is represented as practicing deception, or who permits the shifting of moral responsibility to another, will make no appeal to us. To many people it seems immoral to picture God as fierce and vengeful and as one who needs to be appeased by the blood of a victim. We cannot think of God as a peevish king or feudal monarch, nor of atonement as the propitiation of an angry monarch God. We feel a moral revulsion at the thought of sinners in the hands of a wrathful God. The vicarious principle must be central in all true living, but many conceptions which are set forth in terms such as blood atonement, expiation, ransom, substitution, satisfaction, election, predestination, and the like, have not only lost much of their meaning, but they offend the enlightened moral sense of today. We are touched, however, at the thought of a loving God vicariously suffering for the redemption of men and the progress of the world.

Man cannot think of God as "over yonder," nor apart from the universe watching over it, nor in a state of rest and blessedness. God is in the very structure of the universe. He is taking some part in the religious and moral life which men are now living. We admire those who are willing to help carry the burdens of others and we feel a sense of satisfaction when we share the sufferings and cares of our fellowmen. We cannot think of God as witnessing the woes of humanity without allying Himself with men in their struggles.

Man discovers within himself ideals and aspirations which he is ever striving to fulfill. The consciousness of these ideals and goals creates in him a sense of obligation. Sensitive men feel a moral defeat or inner disharmony when they fail to respond to the sense of obligation. Sin in man seems to be in part a failure to choose and to act upon the highest motive or to select the greatest value in view. In the light of the possible better, man sees the evil nature of the worse, and self-condemnation may result. Much sin also grows out of the social conditions under which men live. Man's life is so bound up with the lives of all human beings, and public evils are so interwoven among our social practices, that no member of society can avoid coming under the effect of numerous great social sins and being partly responsible for them. Man is not only responsible for his own sins, but in a very real sense he is responsible for the sins of others. No man liveth and no man sinneth unto himself. Any explanation of sin which seeks to interpret it as having entered the race through one act, or through one man, thousands of years ago, is unsatisfactory and contrary to the facts of life.

The significance of guilt, punishment, and forgiveness, must be viewed in the light of man's moral outlook. Man feels a sense of guilt when he violates some inner demand of his own life or some social standard which he has come to accept. Punishment that is moral must be remedial in some sense. It ought to create a sense of the unworthiness of the act and a desire to repudiate the past and strive after things which are higher. Just as sin, guilt, and punishment find their meaning in a recognition of a conflict between man's ideals and his actual motives and deeds, so forgiveness finds its meaning in the removal of this sense of conflict. Forgiveness involves a repudiation of the lower motives and deeds and a determination to seek the higher and better. It embraces all the restorative processes by which life moves forward.

Salvation must be viewed as in some sense moral progress. The modern man does not feel that he needs to be saved from the wrath of an angry God. He does need to be saved from many things including ignorance of himself and his relation to his fellowmen and to his environment, from all the things which tend to drag him down and prevent the development of his better self. Salvation interpreted as an external substitutionary transaction is repugnant. To interpret atonement other than as embracing the idea of the setting right of a wrong, or a moral rectification, would be to deny the sanctity of our moral obligations and our sense of right and wrong.

Paul's doctrine of "Justification by Faith Alone" appears to make morality quite incidental to the religious life and to imply that "faith" justifies one in God's sight quite apart from his moral integrity and maturity. This would seem to be a dangerous doctrine to defend. Paul's statement in Ephesians II, 8, "For by grace have ye been saved through faith; and that not of yourselves, it is the gift of God," was taken and written into creeds, without a similar emphasis, such as Paul had made, on moral righteousness. Those who are familiar with the writings of Paul will recall that they are full of moral injunctions. This emphasis on faith alone seems to stand in contrast to the Christian way of life as Jesus portrayed and lived it. For Jesus, salvation meant continuous moral regeneration and growth in the knowledge and likeness of God. The condition for entrance into the Kingdom of God, was, according to Jesus, that a man hunger and thirst after righteousness. "Except your righteousness shall exceed the righteousness of the scribes and Pharisees, ye shall in no wise enter the kingdom of heaven."

Ethical Religion

The most effective way to eliminate unethical religion is to promote ethical religion. Half religion is often a more dangerous foe of religion than either agnosticism or atheism because it lulls people into a sense of complacency. To be religious is not enough; our religion must be of a certain quality or kind. Just what are some of the characteristics of a mature ethical religion? Let us consider the following suggestions as to the kind of religion we need.

First, *we need a religion that appeals to the best in man's entire nature, a religion that is not only felt and thought out, but one that is also lived out.* Religion ought to call forth the response of a man's whole being to that upon which his life depends, or to his object of highest loyalty. It ought not to occupy itself exclusively with any one part of his life.

The emotional element has been prominent in religion. Is religion mainly something that makes us feel good or that stirs our emotions? Some persons have attempted to interpret religion in terms of emotion. Schleiermacher, for example, said that religion is a feeling of absolute dependence upon God. Pure religion, he said, is pure feeling. While Schleiermacher, in our opinion, gave a very one-sided definition of religion, he did religion a service by making clear its mystic inwardness and by saving it from a sterile intellectualism. In religion there are undoubtedly feelings of dependence, of attachment, of commitment, of loyalty, and of fellowship. Without emotion in life there would be no great loves, loyalties, aspirations, ideals, and values.

While the emotional element is important, ethical religion is not merely emotional. Emotions run into great danger of getting lost or sidetracked, unless they are accompanied by reflection. Emotion alone cannot define what it feels, nor communicate its feeling, nor defend its interpretations. These require the use of concepts, of language, and the power of discrimination between that which is true and that which is false. Emotions also may play serious tricks on us. They lead to what the psychologists call mechanisms of escape, of rationalization, of projection, and of compensation. Again, emotionally-toned words may lead us astray, since we may become attached to mere words or phrases rather than to their meanings. A religion of a purely emotional type has often been used to sooth people into inactivity or to keep them in ignorance or in subjection. Emotion in itself is morally neutral; it may be good or evil depending upon the attitude expressed or the things to which it is attached. Our emotions and feelings need to be trained and controlled. We need drive or energy back of our intelligence.

Religion ought to be thought out as well as felt. It ought to be intellectually respectable in the sense that it is in harmony with man's knowledge and outlook. A glance back over history will indicate that the "I believe" element has been very prominent. Some men have even been put to death for not believing as other men thought they should. Some persons have interpreted religion almost exclusively in terms of intellect and belief. Hegel thought that religion was a kind of popular philosophy. It was essentially knowledge possessed by man of his relation to the absolute. Tylor, the anthropologist, said that it was belief in spiritual beings.

What part do knowledge and intellectual elements play in religion? To my way of thinking, they are essential to any high or ethical religion. Without intelligence one could have no doctrines and no intellectual explanations. If a man refuses to reason in the field of religion, it usually means that he has merely fallen back upon the results of the thinking of someone else. Men who are "good" in a traditional sense, but who lack intelligence often do much harm in the world. Religious zeal without intelligence is likely to lead to bigotry and fanaticism. A religion that is not intellectually respectable to modern persons gradually loses its appeal. In an age when thinking is characterized by scientific attitudes and methods, it is essential that religion come to terms with the facts and with the implications of current knowledge.

Just as there is danger in a purely emotional religion, there is danger in a religion of pure intellect. Religion is not merely believing. "Devils may believe and tremble but go on with their devilish ways." Religion is not merely philosophy, nor is it the acceptance of some creed. Intelligence apart from deep ethical and spiritual commitments may enable men to stand aside from the pulsing life of their time. Intelligence which is not committed to a great cause may be harmful and dangerous.

Feeling and intelligence must pass through the crucible of the will if they are to come to fruition in ethical religion. Emotion and intelligence need to translate themselves into man's everyday life of action. Religion is essentially a way of life. It is life of a certain quality or kind. It is a quest for the best kind of life that can be lived in this kind of world. Ethical religion represents the desire of men to put their aspirations and ideals into practice.

In the Old Testament Micah tells us that religion is "To love mercy, to do justly, and to walk humbly with thy God." James, in the New Testament, says that "Pure religion and undefiled before God and the Father is this. To visit the fatherless and widows in their affliction and to keep himself unspotted from the world." Jesus says, "Not every one that saith unto me, Lord, Lord, shall enter into the kingdom of heaven; but he that doeth the will of my Father which is in heaven." Jesus placed supreme emphasis upon life, life of a certain quality, and not upon ritual and creeds. He was concerned with the things that affected life. He approved whatever made for rich and radiant living, and condemned whatever tended to mar life. Religion to him was a vital, first-hand, personal experience. Ethical religion follows him in his devotion to the values of life.

Second, *we need a religion that unites men everywhere in a genuine fellowship and that makes them better rather than worse.* Christianity, with its doctrines of the brotherhood of man and the fatherhood of God, ought to unite men in a great bond of fellowship. Yet it seems clear that some religions have actually separated and divided persons. How unfortunate it is that even one Irishman is reported to have said: "Would to God we were all atheists, so that we could live together like Christians." What bitterness and what conflicts have been generated by immature religious ideals. The writer of the book of Jonah was protesting against a narrow, exclusive religion that refused to share the good things of life with other people.

For centuries there has been evident a drive in the direction of greater unity and equality among men. This drive has tended to break down the barriers of property, class, race, sex, and religion. It is based on the desire of men for a larger life and upon their conception of the worth of human personality. In spite of differences of various kinds men possess in their common humanity something which is worth preserving. The things which unite men and women seem to be more important than those things which divide them. From the Christian point of view men are equal in that they have the right to develop the highest potentialities in their nature.

The story of every great church and denomination is adorned with some pure and noble lives and fragrant with the spirit of devotion and self-sacrifice. The divine river is too large and too broad to be confined by any ecclesiastical banks. Men do not have to think alike nor to feel alike to join in genuine fellowship. Just as it takes all the colors of the spectrum to make the clear sunlight, so men of different capacities and reactions may join to make a better world. A writer in the Jewish Talmud says that one day he was walking on the mountain and saw a form that he took to be a beast. Drawing nearer, he saw it was a man. Drawing nearer still, he found it was his brother. Ethical religion leads men to broaden their understanding and sympathies and to share the values of life with others.

In a previous chapter, we pointed out that men are not morally mature until the in-group comes to include humanity, or until they learn to find their happiness in ways that make happiness possible for all men and women. Can ethical religion demand anything less for its ideal? Ethical religion, while recognizing the depth and extent of sin and guilt, has faith in human nature, in the universe, and in God.

Third, *we need a religion that is growing and dynamic.* Growth, as we have pointed out, is one of the first laws of life. Apparently nothing in man's life, nor in the outer universe, can be conceived as having sprung full-grown. During the last century thinking has changed from that of *being* to that of *becoming*. We have spoken of growth as a mark of a mature morality. If we are not to have a constant lack of harmony between morality and religion, then religion, too, must be dynamic.

While religion has a rich heritage from the past it ought not to be defined simply in terms of its past. Some critics of religion would like to identify it with superstition, or magic, or taboos. This would be like condemning chemistry because of early alchemy. Apart from the fact that religion did not begin in these ways, we cannot emphasize too strongly that "a thing is what it is" and "what it may become," not what it was once. While an account of origins is important, if a thing is in a process of growth the later stages tell more about its nature than do the earlier stages.

Ethical religion is forward-looking in its outlook. It is not completely satisfied with what *is*. It presses toward a possible better. It is expanding and experimental, rather than static and chained to the past or even to the present. It represents the desires of men to make their dreams and ideals become realities. As men grow, not only the "means" they use, but the very ends or goals of life itself grow and expand.

Fourth, *we need a religion that attempts to transform the world in which we live*. Since we shall consider the social program of the church later in this chapter, and some of the social implications of a mature morality in the next chapter, we shall not discuss this topic at length at this point. An ethical religion is not resigned to the world as it is, but is an expression of a determination to change it. When persons are genuinely concerned about the lives of other persons, they are compelled to give attention to the social conditions under

which they live. For example, the early missionaries went to
the distant parts of the earth with a simple, individual gospel.
Since they needed the Bible, they were forced to translate it
into the native language. Since so few persons could read,
they felt the necessity of establishing schools. Since so many
persons became sick and the death rate was high, they became
interested in sanitation and medicine. Since there was much
hunger and poverty, they saw the need of helping the natives
with their agricultural and industrial problems. Almost against
their wills, they were forced to give attention to the social
situation as well as to the "souls" of men. The two could not
be wholly separated.

To starve in the midst of plenty is certainly an evil thing.
To enjoy comforts and luxury in the midst of starvation may
be even more evil and more devastating to the human spirit.
Men can find salvation for themselves only as they seek to
"save" others. Jesus was interested in the social, economic,
and political conditions of his day, not because he lacked
interest in individual men and women, but precisely because
he was deeply interested in them.

Fifth, *we need a religion that links men with that in the
universe which is "life-giving, beauty-making, truth-revealing, and personality-producing."* Men live in a universe that
is pulsing with life and energy. They are part of an on-going
process that existed before they were born and which will
continue. Before they can act or think, or even exist, they
have to accept what is already given by nature. They are
constantly taking advantage of resources which are beyond
their power. This is true whether they plant a garden, go on
a journey, or write a book. In this same universe men feel
an upward urge, a resurgence of life, a creative synthesis.
This is seen wherever love is struggling against hate, goodwill against strife, justice against injustice; wherever knowl-

edge is banishing ignorance or fighting disease; wherever art
is struggling for creative expression; and wherever men are
worshipping an ethical God. There is a trend toward beauty,
toward truth, and toward goodness.

Men may, it is true, resist these trends, or they may co-
operate and share in them. When men do respond they seem
to be moving with the emergent life of the universe. They
may feel the pull of life most strongly in nature's great out-
of-doors, from contact with persons singly or in groups, or
when they are musing alone or meditating upon the heritage
of the past or the call of the future. In whatever form it
comes there is a power beckoning human life in the direction
of the higher. Ethical religion is the kind of devotion that
quickens us in all our upward endeavors. If we can earnestly
believe that the world is of such a nature that it supports our
highest values when right relations are made with it, then we
gain a confidence that can make life radiant. Ethical religion
attempts to instill in men the consciousness that they may be
co-workers with a creative good will. God is no distant being.
"In Him we live and move and have our being."

The Church and Society

Just as man's wish for social order has taken practical
form in the government and the state, and his desire for sexual
expression and parenthood have expressed themselves in the
family, so man's aspirations for guidance and worship and for
an understanding of the meaning of existence have expressed
themselves in the church. Along with the home and the school,
the church is one of the basic institutions in the formation of
character. It plays an important part in helping to lift the
moral level of society. Frequently, however, the church has
been hampered by three things. First, some of its moral codes

were formulated under very simple conditions of life, and their application today presents difficult problems. Second, as established institutions, the churches are closely linked to a social and economic order which is disintegrating. The financial support of the church comes rather largely from the privileged classes that oppose change. Under these conditions, will the church be able to assume leadership in social reconstruction, or is its moral outlook bound up too closely with the preservation of the *status quo*? Third, church membership has been made so easy that it has become largely a convention among some religious bodies. Too many of its members are living in comfortable regions far from the moral frontiers of our civilization. They are not animated by a passion to resist a pagan order which makes a mockery of Christian ideals. To gain adherents, some of the anti-democratic forces are using the word "Christian" in the names or titles of their organizations or publications.

Whereas institutional religion is likely to support the forces of reaction and repression, prophetic and ethical religion will recognize itself as a constructive force for social progress. Prophetic Christianity sees religion as a way of life in which there is a synthesis between personal and social redemption. It wants to save men where they are lost and it recognizes that there is a close relation between personal disintegration and social defeat. Unemployment, lack of food, inadequate housing, and lack of medical care, among other things, may make the redemptive process difficult. Just because religion is "person centered" it cannot disregard any condition that destroys persons.

The social program of the church, which is an expression of an ethical religion, may well include the following: first, an attempt to build a mature social conscience in its members. This will include the creation of an attitude that condemns social injustices as well as personal sins. Since the church includes to some extent a cross-section of society and persons at all stages of intellectual and ethical development, the average level of life and action cannot be as high as that of some smaller groups within its membership. Where the church is united it should move forward and exert pressure as rapidly as the moral judgment of its members will support action. The church must keep alive man's faith in a better world.

Second, the church can aid in the ethical analysis of contemporary problems and challenge its members, doctors, lawyers, teachers, business men, laborers, and farmers, to find the meaning of Christian ethics for the particular groups of which they are members. The churches will not be able to formulate details of business or professional procedure, but they ought to be able to formulate principles of procedure and to urge that these be followed.

Third, the church can supply much volunteer service to aid the constructive agencies in the community and it can send out its members, inspired by high ideals, to engage in activities which the church as a whole may not be able to support. The actual conduct of "social welfare" or "social service" work by churches is probably not the most effective service. Social welfare work is not necessarily more adequate if carried on under church auspices. In fact, experience seems to indicate that it is done most effectively by those agencies which give their entire attention to such work. There is also a danger that "social service" work is carried on by some wealthy churches as a compensation for an anti-social attitude on the part of the members. It may represent an attempt to mitigate the evils of the present order instead of an attempt to discover whether changes ought to be made in the order itself.

Fourth, the church can bring its influence to bear by insisting upon the use of just methods in social change. The church ought to insist upon the use of peaceful, reasonable, and democratic methods in so far as they conform to the realities of the situation confronted. That this procedure is not always easy the following quotation will indicate: "We have heard much of nonviolent resistance as an ethical method, but there is an evil form of overtly nonviolent resistance by intrenched privilege which can afford to forego aggression. It has no need of violence because it possesses the resources to prevent the working classes, by deadly, quiet resistance, from attaining a more abundant life. In the face of such resistance the church cannot justly turn away from a rebellious class or group simply because in desperation it resorts to force. A Christian judgment upon violence must begin with the spiritual violence that begets physical battle. Christianity is deeply and invariably committed to the method of love, in the sense of active good will, but to enjoin its use upon men whom elemental need has forced into unequal struggle, while taking no steps to remove the injustice which has incited them to revolt, is to uphold the hand of the exploiter." [8]

The church can be the source of constant ferment in society ever pointing men to something better. When it is impossible for men to make a completely good choice, because of previous mistakes and evils, they should be encouraged to do the thing which is relatively most just in the situation. The church can also help people to start living right now the attitude that belongs to the better world for which men of good will are striving. It can insist upon those conditions in society which are essential for the development of persons of moral integrity and religious devotion.

CHAPTER VII

IMPLICATIONS FOR PRESENT-DAY SOCIETY

CERTAIN MARKS OF a mature morality or certain principles for living have been set forth. To state such principles is one thing; it is quite another thing to apply them to the structure of the society in which we live. A moral issue is never just a moral problem; it is also a problem of personal choice, of economics, of politics, or of international relations. A moral truth or an ideal is never completely learned and understood until men are actually engaged in the struggle of putting it into practice. A considerable part of the moral inertia of our age is due to the superficial faith which so many persons have in good resolutions. Moral ideas do not and cannot secure their own fulfillment. The fundamental conflict of our time is the glaring gap between our ideals and the lives we live from day to day, between our loyalties and the demands of the social situation. Unless we are attempting to reconstruct our society, we cannot be sure of "saving" ourselves. There is a tremendous contrast between what human life is today, and what it might be even on the basis of the knowledge and the instrumentalities we already have. The statement is sometimes made, with a considerable degree of justification, that the social problem has "piled up" in recent decades due to the rapidly accelerating pace of social change. We face "collapse or reconstruction." To drift is to court disaster.

We have already pointed out that society is undergoing rapid changes. Even under more normal conditions, it is of the nature of social life to grow and to expand. Some parts of the social mechanism tend to change more rapidly than others. When this happens there is likely to be tension and conflict. Social "problems" arise which demand attention. To answer the question as to *why* changes are occurring so rapidly would require more space than is available, as the contributing factors are many and varied. Take, for example, the one fact of inventions. From about 100 A. D. to 1400 A.D., there were practically no significant advances in technology, but since then they have been rapid. The discovery or application of the use of gunpowder was a factor in the decline of feudalism. A series of inventions in the seventeenth and early eighteenth centuries, including the steam engine, led to the decline of the domestic or handicraft system and the coming of the industrial revolution. Now, literally thousands of inventions are patented every year in the United States alone. Whether we like it or not, because of the automobile, the aeroplane, the radio, the joint stock company, and thousands of other inventions, physical and social, we are in the midst of an unintended revolution.

The most urgent question before us now relates to the social goals toward which we should move. New social philosophies have arisen and their adherents are striving to gain our allegiance and support. If, as a people, we are not to be carried away with glittering generalities and false utopias, we need to make clear our social, political, and economic objectives. Loss of moral and spiritual goals is more serious than a reduction of national income. Once America stood as the great experimental ground of new ideals and her citizens had the thrill of feeling that they were building a new civilization. Does it appear that other nations with new and somewhat strange philosophies are gaining the thrill of achievement and are feeling a sense of urgency in building a new civilization?

The Democratic Ideal

A mature morality implies an acceptance of the democratic ideal in contrast to other forms of political control. The democratic way of life rests essentially on moral foundations, whereas the fascist or totalitarian conception is a denial of basic postulates of morality. To make this clear, let us consider four basic assumptions underlying the democratic way.

First, democracy is based on the assumption and conviction of the worth and dignity of all men. Man, just because he is a person, or a self, with self-consciousness, intelligence, and the ability to distinguish between right and wrong, is an end in himself. Only in a person do we have a center of feeling with joys and sorrows. There is no good in human life except the satisfaction of human needs. If the individual possesses worth, his personality is not to be violated. He is not to be exploited for the gain of others.

Democracy is based on a faith that the things which all men have in common, that is, their basic selfhood including self-consciousness and the power of reflection, are more important than those superficial distinctions of race, color, class or economic standing. It is also based upon faith in the capacities of the common man, that he has great possibilities or potentialities, and that he can be educated.

Human freedom is an implication of this postulate of the worth of each individual person. Man ought to be free to think and to express his thoughts. Take away man's freedom and he becomes something less than a man. If men cannot think and express their thoughts it is not very long before they have no thoughts worth expressing. They tend to become docile "yes-men." They become something less than well-rounded, fully-developed personalities.

These convictions concerning the worth and dignity of all men, and concerning human freedom, stand in sharp contrast to the view that the state is supreme or total. These assumptions are true for democracy and for a mature Christian morality. Their acceptance would shatter completely the fascist or totalitarian ideal, as we have seen.

Second, *democracy is based on the assumption of the desirability of popular control over basic issues of policy.* This is the view that every man knows more about what his desires and needs are than does someone else. Therefore, he ought to have some say, or some right to criticize. In popular language, "Only the wearer of the shoe knows where it pinches." Those who have to obey laws ought to have a voice in making them and in electing the officials who enforce them. The majority ought to determine the policy on major issues. "What affects all should have the consent of all." Legislative bodies and executive leaders must be responsible to the expressed will of the majority, but the minority must be heard and protected.

A further implication of the democratic way is that human affairs can be settled best by discussion and reason. In the long run people would rather be governed less efficiently and govern themselves than efficiently but without freedom. Irresponsible power tends to be used in the interest of the group that possesses it. If leaders are cut off from the people and from criticism, they lose touch with them, and it is not very long before the rulers are ruling in their own interests. Abraham Lincoln was right when he said, "No man is good enough or wise enough to govern another man without his consent." Democracy implies the right of the minority to become the majority if it is able to do so by the peaceful processes of persuasion.

Democracy rests upon a concept of society and a concept

of government that are distinctive. The concept of society is that the purpose of organized society is the well-being, the happiness, the personal development of the individual human beings who make up the group. The concept of government is that government should be vested in the people whom it is designed to benefit. The best guarantee, perhaps the only guarantee, that power or authority will be used for the benefit of the people is to vest that power in *all* the people.

In the early days, after the earlier settlers came to Massachusetts the people met together in "Town Meetings" to make their decisions. That direct form of democracy can still be carried on in small communities and in small groups. As the population grew, it became necessary to elect delegates or representatives to act for the people. Political "machinery" tended to accumulate. The abuses and problems of democracy have had to do with the machinery of democracy rather than with its basic ideals.

Third, *democracy is based on the assumption that this is the kind of world that can be made better and that the average citizens have a responsibility in helping to reconstruct society.* This is not a superficial optimism. Few intelligent persons can be very optimistic about the world today. On the other hand, it is not pessimism. Certainly not the pessimism that so easily leads to cynicism and inactive despair. The position is sometimes called "meliorism," a word that means "better" or "betterment." The conception implies that this is a world that can be made better and that we have a responsibility to do something about it. This is what has been meant by the American Doctrine of Progress. It implies growth in moral insight and ideals. It is also in harmony with what Christians have called the coming of the Kingdom of God.

Under the democratic way, changes ought to be: (1)

Conscious social changes by consent. They ought to come after discussion and deliberation, and not as the result of force, of emotional outbursts, or of propaganda or trickery. (2) Changes guided or directed by the use of intelligence. Democracy, as we have seen, implies faith in the intelligence of the average citizens and a disposition to abide by the results of that reflection.

This conviction that life can be made better means that all that mars human personality is destined to go. Poverty, unemployment, slums, crime, and violence stand condemned along with other evils. Perhaps the only way to save civilization is to keep trying to improve it.

Fourth, *democracy implies that as gains and improvements arise they ought to be widely distributed among the people.* Some of our so-called progress has benefited only a section of the population. Recently we have heard much talk about the bottom third of the population that is ill-fed, ill-clothed, and ill-housed. We have failed most woefully in the application of this assumption. If large sections of the population have little share in the products of society, if they have little or nothing to lose by sweeping changes in society, they provide fertile ground for the growth of social panaceas and revolutionary social philosophies which would break our connection with the past and lead to a doubtful future.

The concept of "the general welfare" has been prominent in democratic literature and discussions. The constitution of the United States was established to promote, among other things, the welfare of the citizens. "We, the people of the United States, in order to form a more perfect union . . ., promote the general welfare, and secure the blessings of liberty . . . do ordain and establish this constitution. . . ." The strong are not to exploit the weak, but are to help bear their burdens. A fairly general equality of conditions is a foundation stone of popular government. We shall consider this problem further in a later section.

In addition to these assumptions underlying democracy, there are certain conditions necessary for a really successful democracy. For example, there need to be certain qualities of character in the individual citizens. These include a high degree of moral responsibility and self-control and a high degree of social sympathy and co-operativeness. There needs to be a willingness to work with and for other people and to share common interests and purposes, to enter appreciatively and sympathetically into the lives of others and to see their problems. For a successful democracy, an informed and educated group of citizens is essential. Without this, freedom may be abused. Again, democracy is adapted to peace rather than to the conditions of war. Democracies find it harder to develop the lust for conquest. They tend to cultivate the virtues and spirit of peace rather than those of war. While the dictators have a temporary advantage in a time of crisis or war, healthy democracies probably have more staying power, and morale is less likely to crack under strain.

Democracy is not dependent upon any one set or type of political institutions. The principle of representative government is older than our present political institutions and will outlive them. The forms have been changing. For example, we have changed from indirect to direct representation in the Senate, the primaries, and in the election of the president. These statements are not meant to minimize political machinery and our responsibility for making democracy work better. Many things need to be done to improve the working of our political institutions. Set up in the eighteenth century under quite different conditions, some of these institutions are not working well today. Men of intelligence and good will ought to put forth every effort to eliminate the spoils system, patronage, nepotism, inefficiency, fraud or corruption, and the "political machines" which exercise a selfish control over primaries, conventions, and the like. On the other hand, we might well consider an extension of the civil service, the separation of the administration of justice and other functions from control by party politics, and the shorter ballot. Modern conditions, including the rise of statistical methods that enable the accurate polling of public opinion and the wide use of the radio, would seem to indicate a need for a reconsideration of the problems of centralization and decentralization. The penalty which good men pay for their lack of interest and lack of a sense of responsibility in their government is that they are likely to be governed by men who are worse than themselves.

Democracy is a way of life and a theory of character; it is not merely a form of government or a political philosophy. The democratic ideal must become an actuality in the daily affairs of men. It includes the right of men to think, to speak, to write, to vote, and to participate in the functions of government. But it includes much more than these rights. It includes economic democracy in which one individual must not exploit another individual and in which there is economic security for all. Democracy implies a wide diffusion of property and wealth. Great distinctions of wealth and income are detrimental to a democracy. Democracy includes cultural democracy in which all persons have an opportunity to share in the cultural and spiritual heritage of the past, including art, science, philosophy, literature, and religion. Unless men can satisfy and express these aspirations and functions they fall short of happiness and self-realization. Today because of educational, class, and economic barriers, great masses of people are deprived of these cultural advantages. Democracy as a way of life also includes racial democracy in which men shall not be subject to discrimination merely on account of color or race. A report, published a few years ago by The Institute for Propaganda Analysis, stated that there were numerous fascist or near-fascist organizations in the United States carrying on anti-Semitic propaganda. Racial prejudice is responsible for much baseness and cruelty and for many warped lives.

Democracy does not imply that individual differences are to be eliminated. Persons vary in their physical, intellectual, and spiritual characteristics. Democracy may well cherish these differences for the contributions they may make toward a richer common life. As persons, however, all men have a right to the conditions, in so far as they are available, which make possible the development of their potentialities. The ideals of liberty, equality, and human brotherhood must be more than emotionally-toned words. They must become realities in terms of good health, adequate housing, freedom of conscience, knowledge, education, participation in the determination of the political and industrial conditions of life, and a share in the rich cultural heritage of the race.

Economic Relationships

Some of the most serious problems facing modern society have to do with the working of our economic institutions. No one planned the system and few persons are pleased with the way it is working. Our economic practices have grown up, rather haphazardly, with little or no conscious attention apart from the fact that most men were striving to make money in their special fields. Business success, rather than principles of Christian morality, has been the guiding force.

In the days of the early settlers, men owned the simple tools which they used and they usually had title to the land on which they worked. Agricultural pursuits were predominant. Men worked in or near the home. They had ready access to raw material, and any energetic, able-bodied man could support himself, his wife, and his family. Moreover, there was, until about 1890, an open frontier with amazing opportunities, and an ever-expanding market.

One of the most revolutionary changes in human relations has taken place as a result of the "Industrial Revolution" and the triumphant march of natural science and technology. Industry has superseded agricultural pursuits. Machinery, factories, specialization, production for profit, credit and banking, joint stock corporations, separation of owners and managers, concentration of wealth have become the order of the day. Without ownership of the tools, work is insecure. Without work, the masses cannot eat. Underlying a considerable portion of contemporary unrest is the desire of men for that more abundant living which they believe is possible.

Owing to the increasing concentrations of economic power, and in spite of democratic forms, the system has been operated for the benefit of a comparatively small group in control at the top. The bottom layers in our society are the victims of our economic "progress." Large sections of the population feel that they need emancipation, not so much from their political leaders, but from the arbitrariness and ruthlessness of their economic rulers who resort to coercion, espionage, and sabotage to prevent the masses from sharing in the vast material and cultural wealth that is available. By means of excessive prices to consumers and financial rewards to insiders, the gains of economic progress and the fruits of science and technology have been siphoned off and kept from passing on to the people. If this is not as true today as a decade or two ago, it is largely due to the effectiveness of recent governmental control measures.

While much remains to be done in the improvement and adaptation to new conditions of our political institutions, much more remains to be done on the economic side, if we are to follow the democratic ideal. Too frequently we have permitted the few to control the means by which the many must live. Consequently, "liberty" may be merely liberty to starve. Instead of democracy, we have permitted the growth of autocracy. Instead of equality of opportunity in the economic field, we have permitted privilege and power to get into the hands of small groups. Private monopoly tends to deny the substance of freedom, democracy, and equality of opportunity. We have moved toward dictatorship through money power. A serious danger is that men who desire freedom and security and food may come to choose security and food without freedom rather than suffer privation. Men who have little or no stake in the present social order may easily be persuaded to try something different. Fascism has arisen where democracy has failed to meet basic human needs or to give men hope for the future.

For years, before our "all out" defense measures, the nation suffered from an abundance of idle machinery, idle money, and idle men. If we do not constructively use our machines, our money, and our man power, it is obvious that the nation is economically sick or in trouble. The crisis is due in part to the dominance of certain ideas which are embedded in our industrial order; some of these ideas were mentioned in chapter one. There is the doctrine of self-interest, that there must be opportunity for unrestricted personal gain. It may express itself in terms of the profit motive, that profit is the only effective incentive, or in terms of the "economic man" who is without altruistic impulses in his business activities. There are also the doctrines of "free competition," of the right to unlimited private property, and of individualism or *laissez-faire*. A man, it is claimed, has a right to all the money and power he is able to get and there should be no interference by the government or by society.

These ideas are responsible for much of our "economic immorality." In a simple society, characterized by intimate, personal relations, they worked fairly well. In our modern complex society, they are leading to domestic anarchy and to international chaos. So long as the purpose of industry is not to satisfy basic human needs, but is considered as a game played in the immediate financial interests of the individual players, we shall have unemployment, poverty, and widespread misery with the constant danger of disorder, revolution, and war.

In pointing out that he cannot reconcile capitalism with a mature morality or with Christianity, the Dean of Canterbury says, "Our system lacks moral basis. It is only justified on the grounds that no alternative exists. It gives rise, when Christian men and women accept it and acquiesce in it, to that fatal divergence between principles and practice of Christian people, which is so damning to religion, and which found its sternest critic in Christ himself. The gap between Sunday, with its sermons on brotherhood, co-operation, seeking of others' good, and Monday, with its competitive rivalries, its veiled warfares, its concentration upon acquisition, its determination to build up one's own security, becomes so wide that many of the better men and women of today remain outside the churches altogether. Hypocrites they will not be. The young especially, with their modern passion for sincerity, are in open revolt." [1]

Again he says, "No longer must the livelihood of the community rest in irresponsible hands; blast furnaces remaining cold, mines undug, and houses unbuilt, unless somebody's private profit sets forward the lighting, the digging, and the building. Shivering miners cannot dig the coal they need; naked men cannot weave their own shirts and coats, nor can the man who lives seven in a single room enter a brickyard and build himself a house; though he kick his heels for a dozen years in idleness, he must remain in misery if no one can make a profit from his labour. The public that needs these things and can produce them has no access to the land and the machinery of production. Private profit takes precedence of human life. Christian morality, if it is to be true to its mission, must find these things intolerable and demand their reform." [2]

Since the medieval period there has been a remarkable reversal of values. The earlier sins of pride, avarice, greed, usury, and luxury have tended, with the rise of capitalism, to become cardinal virtues. Pride, once regarded as the greatest of sins, has become pride in wealth, in class, in birth, and in the nation. Avarice has become the virtue of thrift. Usury is the reward for risk and for deferred satisfaction. Today it may be called "interest," although the term "usury" is more often used for an exorbitant rate of interest. Luxury is held before men as a motive for greater effort. Instead of morality restraining and controlling the great machines of power, power has tended to demoralize life and to set its own standards. [3] Is it any wonder that resentment, callousness, selfish nationalism, militarism, economic imperialism, and war have been the result? Fascism or totalitarianism is merely the final form of the drive for power and possession.

A society that is ethically mature will stress and develop the motives that are social, and not put a halo around selfishness and acquisitiveness. While we may need to enlist the self-regarding motives, we must not overstress them to the exclusion of other drives. Other ages have gotten along without the profit motives, and in society today large groups of people are dominated by other incentives. If many persons, or most persons, today are dominated by the drive to get rich, that is no reason why this is human nature or that it must be so. When the appeal is sufficiently strong, men respond to appeals to public service. We need to develop more fully than we have in the past such incentives to action as loyalty, creativity, love, public approval, and recognition, etc. We tend to do the thing which the group we respect expects us to do.

Society is economically as well as socially interdependent. It is becoming increasingly clear that the welfare of each individual and group is indissolubly bound up with the welfare of other individuals and groups. Never was it more true than today that no man liveth or dieth unto himself alone. The economic welfare of the once independent farmer and of the business man is bound up with world economic conditions. The only adequate defense of the good life for anyone is to make it available to all men and women. Both from the point of view of good ethics and good economics there ought to be a wider distribution of purchasing power, for without this, the system itself is not likely to survive.

Regarding the economic order in which we live, the following three statements seem to be in order. First, the principle of private enterprise is fairly deeply embedded in the American mentality. It arose under quite different conditions and was connected with doctrines that are now obsolete. Probably a great majority of Americans feel that a considerable degree of freedom of economic enterprise is essential to the maintenance of their heritage of freedom, and that there are some areas in which private enterprise and competition will continue to serve the public welfare most adequately. These fields will undoubtedly include the small businesses, the novelty and luxury trade, new enterprises, and the crafts in which individual skill is the important element. Private enterprise is not in principle immoral, but it has frequently led to excesses which are immoral.

Belief in the sanctity of private property is also fairly strong. What ethical justification does it have? If we examine the arguments for private property set forth in the past, it is evident that users' or consumers' property is generally the type which is in mind. If private property for use is an instrument in the development of the best life, then the advantages of ownership ought to be widely diffused throughout society. An examination of the indictment of private property will indicate that it is usually another type of property, property for power or the private ownership of the great instruments of production, which is under attack. We need more private property in consumers' or users' goods, such as homes, food, clothing, and the like, and less private property in the means by which the members of the community live.

Second, it is apparently the part of wisdom to take under public control those functions that are really public in scope. Private monopolies have proved to be too dangerous. In the past, various functions which tended to be monopolistic and which were essential to the welfare of nearly all persons have been taken over by society itself and run as public services. Today more than a score of our most important social functions, from schools to post offices, are operated in this way, and society registers, inspects, or regulates nearly all of the functions left in private hands. Certain functions are too important from the point of view of social welfare, and certain powers are too great to be left in individual hands. Consequently, social ownership and control will probably be, and probably ought to be, extended to take in the great natural resources, including the sources of power, our main systems of communication and transportation, and the power to issue credit and currency. Services which are monopolistic or near-monopolistic should be operated as public services under democratic control or they should be carefully regulated.

Third, a considerable degree of experimentation in the field of our economic relations is desirable. The object of such experimentation will be to discover instrumentalities or ways of doing things that will further promote human welfare. This field of experimentation is likely to be between the areas where public ownership seems most satisfactory and the area where private enterprise functions most adequately. Most Americans wish to avoid the dangers both of too great centralization of governmental functions and of an uncontrolled individualism.

In recent years many consumers' co-operatives have been organized. The principles and practices of the co-operatives seem to satisfy both the idealistic and the practical needs of many persons. They emphasize and develop social-mindedness in that each succeeds only as everyone else succeeds. The principles of a voluntary, unrestricted membership, and one member one vote, are in line with some of the basic assumptions of the democratic way of life and the Christian ethical ideal. Under such a system where the surplus or earnings are returned to the members in proportion to patronage, there is no advantage to be gained in profiteering, in deceptive advertisements, or in distributing a poor quality of merchandise or service. Thus certain evils of our industrial system tend to be checked.

An industrial society which contained public, private, and co-operative activity would not fear stagnation or lack of novelty. Each one would be a stimulus to the others as well as a check upon the abuses that tend to arise in connection with the other two.

Private initiative and individual responsibility will be the dominant elements in certain areas where the individual seems to be more competent to know the facts and to decide the issues. For example, the farmer should retain the initiative in the planting, harvesting, and storing of his crops, the business man in the purchase of quantities of stock for his store. On the other hand, there is an area where the individual will be less competent than some voluntary group which he may join. In the grading and sale of his produce the farmer will need the aid of his co-operative marketing association. The business man is dependent on his trade association to establish trade practice. Finally, there are areas in which neither the individual nor the voluntary group is competent. The state will need to attend to such matters as taxation, tariffs, and the regulations for the collection of debts, as well as the operation of such natural monopolies and public services as the water supply.

The chief function of an industrial system is to provide for the physical needs and well-being of the entire population. In an enlightened democracy, such a system must care for most persons most of the time; otherwise there will be a demand for changes in the system. Institutions are ethically justified only to the degree that they bring the maximum satisfaction of human wants or serve the people more satisfactorily than could any other institutions that are available to replace them. Institutions stand condemned if they fail to meet human needs.

International Relations

The chaos and anarchy of the world today is so evident to all informed persons that a description is not necessary. We have spoken, in previous sections, of certain ideas that are in large part responsible for our "economic immorality." Some of these same ideas, on the international level, are responsible for our "international immorality." The idea of self-interest tends to be raised to the level of the state. In such a case, it becomes national self-interest that leads a nation to act only when its immediate interest or "honor" is at stake. Commercial competition stimulates national rivalry. A nation can have and keep, it is asserted, all the territory that it can get by one means or another. Thus "power politics" is encouraged, as well as the belief that there ought to be no interference with the nation by any League of Nations or superstate or world federation.

In advocating some type of federalism for the world the Archbishop of Canterbury has referred to the close relation between the economic order and world chaos. He says, ". . . I do not believe that a federal system can of itself secure justice or even abolish war unless the economic life of men is ordered on principles more expressive of fellowship than at present. The trend toward war is inherent in the internal economy of the modern nation. The essential evil in the ordering of European life has been the inversion of the proper relations between finance, production and consumption. It is evident that the real object for which goods are produced is that they may be enjoyed, and this in most instances means 'consumed.' The consumer is the factor of primary importance, whose interest ought to be decisive, for his is the only truly human interest in the whole process. Yet food is destroyed while men are hungry. Why? Because they have not the means to make their need constitute a market. So the primary aim of producing food turns out to be in practice, not feeding the hungry, but making a profit. The profit motive has become the dominant motive. It is this which has led to the sacrilegious sacrifice of rural England to urban interests and subjects it to policies framed for urban conditions. It has turned man into an economic animal.

"This leads to a competition for markets, which was comparatively harmless so long as the market was expanding with no visible limit. But that is no longer so. Now the predominance of the profit motive as the mainspring of industry leads to dangerous rivalries, which often contain the threat of war. It is perfectly true that few, if any, industrialists desire war; it is true that for most forms of business war itself is a source of loss rather than profit. It is not the policy of the industrialists but the principle on which industry is organized, which has a tendency toward war.

"Moreover, the system shows signs of ceasing to work. It is unable to provide employment, and therewith the basis for honorable life, to an alarmingly large number of citizens. . . . There are people who want to work and cannot work, because they cannot be 'profitably employed.' Profitably to whom? That their work might be profitable to the nation and to themselves there is no doubt." [4]

While we live in a world of war, practically all men and women want peace and realize the values and need of peace. With the exception of small groups of militarists, men realize that war is a great evil, that unless we eliminate war, war is likely to destroy the finest products of our civilization. There is a growing conviction that war is futile, and that it is wrong to spend such large amounts of money on instruments of destruction when we might use our resources for the promotion of health, education, and a higher economic and cultural standard of living. The present conflict was one of the hardest wars to get started, and when it began there was less fanfare than in the last great war.

Not only do the masses of men and women want peace, but our interdependent world urgently demands peace. Whether we consider it from the point of view of our economic and political problems or from the point of view of our cultural, scientific, and religious contacts, the world is one. Events and the decisions of individuals and groups thousands of miles away affect our lives profoundly. With a provincialism and a parochialism of an age that is past, modern man finds himself thrust into a situation with which he is not able to cope. In the United States, we would have preferred to get along without conscription in peace time, without a Lease-Lend Bill, without having our economy further disrupted, without our minds being disturbed and our nerves being agitated, and without having to engage in global war, but we do live in the world. We are learning with Lowell that "In the gain or loss of one race all the rest have equal claim." Apparently, there is no likelihood that we can solve the problems which we face, except as we do so on a worldwide basis. The world has become a physical neighborhood and our thinking and our morals must recognize this fact.

The main difficulty today is that the world is organized around the concept of national sovereignty and not around the concept of humanity. The world is divided into areas of suspicion, fear, and hatred. There is little difference between the discarded doctrine of the "divine right of kings" and the prevalent doctrine of the "divine right of national sovereignty." The utter immorality of the current world view is seen not only in the global war, but in the fact that it is assumed not only that nations will not act, but that they ought not to act unless their national interests are directly involved. Many men live psychologically in the outlook of a time when physical isolation was almost a reality. For them the nation represents the outer boundary of human concern and sympathy.

At one time there was a "moral law" for all men and nations in the Western "civilized" world. It was by no means perfect, but it was enforced so far as possible by the popes and emperors. Before long, however, the universalism of the medieval period was due to break up into a new particularism. The trend is seen in the rise of the kingly power and the national states. The doctrine of sovereignty arose in the sixteenth century as a justification of the national monarchic state which was then evolving. It served the double purpose of helping to establish the claims of the monarchy above those of the imperial and the papal authorities; and also above the claims of the nobles, the self-governing cities, and the guilds. As expressed in earlier centuries the doctrine set forth the view that the sovereign was supreme, that he was above the law. He made the law but he was not subject to it. With the change in the form of the state from absolute to limited monarchy, then to republicanism and democracy, the doctrine has persisted. Sovereignty means the supreme power of the state expressed in the claims of internal authority and freedom from all external restraint. It is the conception of the state as power, as a law unto itself.

Are we clinging to a conception which has been outgrown? We urgently need international laws, but our traditional conceptions stand in the way of a free development of international law. We need new machinery for handling international disputes and for carrying on international affairs of all kinds. We need a world culture and outlook, but our traditions of nationalism are not compatible with such a development.

The alternatives before us appear to be: (1) To continue

with the present concepts of nationalism and sovereignty and to face even more hideous wars in the future. During recent decades nationalism has been again on the increase with a tendency to place the nation above ethical considerations. (2) To permit one nation or a group of closely allied nations to dominate the world and bring some enforced unity. Such a unity, unless very liberal and humanitarian, is not likely to last long. When nations fear others they begin to arm or to combine against those whom they fear. (3) To build some form of world organization which will recognize the legitimate aspirations of all men and which will provide for peaceful, progressive changes as new conditions and new problems arise.

The third alternative would seem to be in harmony with the principles of a mature morality. Today our interdependent world urgently needs some form of world organization or federation to handle its common problems. The League of Nations, established after the World War, 1914-1918, made an admirable attempt and had some notable accomplishments to its credit, especially in its non-political activities. Its main weaknesses and failures on the political side were due to the uncompromising nationalism of the member states. The main tasks of morally mature men are to discover and to eliminate the causes of war, and to build the public opinion and the institutions that will make possible some form of world federation with sufficient power to keep the peace against outlaw groups and international racketeers.

An immediate ethical problem before men today has to do with the attitude they should take toward participation in war. When their nation is involved in war, whether it is attacked or because vital interests are at stake, what is the mature individual to do? For many the situation is difficult because any choice may seem evil and may involve some compromise. After war has actually started the choice is not one between peace and war, but between victory and defeat. To engage in the terrible task of killing, or to stand aside and see one's country overrun and defeated, is a tragic alternative. Men of apparently equal intelligence and good will may decide differently because they differ in the perspective from which they approach the problem, in technical judgment, and in their prediction of the results of certain actions on the course of future events. A fine example of this is the series of articles by ten Christian leaders, "If America Enters the War What Shall I Do?" *The Christian Century,* December 4, 1940-February 5, 1941. The answers range all the way from an unqualified refusal to participate to an expression of determination to support the nation in war and help to prevent the growth of despotism in the world.

Practically all thoughtful Christians are agreed that war is an evil; that it is a demonstration of the power of sin in the world; and that it must be eliminated from human society as soon as possible. But that agreement does not solve their dilemma as the following statement issued by five Christian pacifists and five non-pacifists will indicate: "There are two judgments which all Christians are called to make concerning a given war. One is the judgment upon the relative right and wrong as between the parties at war. The other is the judgment upon war *per se.* In both judgments concerning this war, virtually all thoughtful Christians are in accord.

"In any particular war the Christian will define his attitude and act according to his view of the comparative weight and urgency of these judgments. One Christian may feel constrained to take up arms; his friend may find himself compelled to take the contrary course. The one may believe that the immediate issues for his fellow men are so great that he cannot refrain from going to their succor, even though he may have to recognize that he may be a party to all the evils of war. The other may believe that he cannot take part in any war, even though he may have to recognize that his abstention may prolong great sufferings." [5]

A pacifist is one who is completely disillusioned about war and its power to produce any good results that are commensurate with the evils involved. This disillusionment has been strengthened by a knowledge of the results of the first World War. He feels that war as a means is so evil that it can lead only to more evil. Therefore he refuses to participate. If he is a Christian he will usually add that the necessary acts of war are irreconcilably opposed to the spirit and teachings of Jesus and to the Christian conception of a loving God. The Christian, he feels, must endeavor to solve the conflicts between nations in some more constructive way. He must "overcome evil with good." If he is told that the way of love frequently fails to achieve its objective, he will reply that the way of force and violence fails even more frequently. Pacifists are likely to emphasize the part which economic imperialism and nationalistic self-interests play in modern wars.

The stand of the pacifist, as stated above, is a moral stand and as such it ought to be respected. The pacifist keeps alive the ideal of a peaceful world. It is an individual way of life which some men will choose. That it is difficult to follow and to maintain is evident by the many conscientious pacifists who have recently changed sides. To refuse to use force under any circumstances might invite criminals to take control. To refuse all use of force against aggression might encourage some dictator looking for easy conquests. After pointing out that pacifism is an actual obligation only for those who see it as a necessary part of their Christian way of life, and a potential obligation for others, C. J. Cadoux, who defends pacifism says: "This means, of course, that—as the world is at present constituted—no political state can very well be pacifist, for no state contains the requisite proportion of convinced pacifists among its citizens. The state has, however, to deal somehow with the crying evils of the world, both within and without its borders; hence it has to exert some measure of injurious coercion on violent criminals and rioters at home, and, at times, it has to wage war against lawless men from abroad—and this because, as a state, it possesses against the transgressors no other weapon in which it trusts as promising sufficient power and promise of success against them. That state of things the pacifist ought frankly to recognize. He ought to abandon once and for all the attempt to show that a completely pacifist policy is open to his or any other nation, the members of which are individually lacking in the one conviction that makes pacifist behavior feasible and right. He ought to go further and recognize that, relative to the mentality of the bulk of his fellow-citizens, violence and war, being sometimes their duty, have in the past and may in the present and future issue in at least partially good results." [6]

The Christian who is a nonpacifist, while realizing the evil of war, thinks that upon occasions it may involve less injustice, tyranny, and evil that any of its present alternatives. He is forced to recognize that in actual conflicts one side is frequently definitely better than the other. In such cases military action may prevent grave injustice. The choice may be one between war and tyranny. He denies that all the wars of history have produced only evil. In some cases they have prevented injustices and defended human rights. Whereas the pacifist is likely to stress the evil of war, the nonpacifist is likely to stress the brutality of modern tyranny and its distortion of the human mind and spirit as well as the subjection of the body.

The nonpacifist Christian does not feel that the ethics of non-resistance of the Sermon on the Mount necessarily justifies an absolute pacifism. Jesus, he may say, believed that the present world order was destined to pass away. While his followers were not to use violence, he did not attribute non-violence to God. God was soon to establish his Kingdom with power, to the consternation of the wicked. When the world did not pass away, and as Christians increased in society and came to occupy positions of responsibility and authority in the state, they began to share the responsibility of defending the community and the state. Many Christians, from different points of view, do not feel that the ethics of the New Testament prevent them from opposing even by the use of force "those who would destroy the values love seeks to create."

Let us make our position clear. There are equally sincere and conscientious people on both sides of this issue. The Christian ought not to surrender his conscience to the state. If a man believes that a war is unjust or wrong, it is his duty to refuse to support it. Those who do not accept his position ought to respect and to defend his right to hold it. If a man feels that war is the lesser evil of the alternatives at a particular time he ought to support it. The church will need to keep before men the need of building a society in which war can be eliminated. Without identifying herself entirely with the pacifist or the soldier, the church must offer her services and ministrations to both groups.

Whenever questions of defense arise, it is important to ask, "What is to be defended?" "Can the things we wish to survive be defended by war or have all other means been tried?" There are many false assumptions prevalent today. One is that we can prevent war merely by agitation for peace. Such agitation, however, may lead men to seek out and remedy the causes of war. Another assumption is that if we remain isolated as a nation all will be well. Recent events should have banished all such notions. We must have a social order before we can make much progress toward the improvement of that order. There is "no peace except as the outgrowth of an order; no enduring order except as it magnifies consent and reduces the appeal to force; no such reduction of the appeal to force, except through the development of a government of greater scope than that of the national state—such are the conclusions to which a consideration of the logic of both pacifist and patriot seems to lead us." [7]

Contemporary Blueprints for Society

Practically all persons, except extreme conservatives and reactionaries, believe that we must build a new and better society. There are many blueprints, many "ways out," that are being suggested. Capitalists, fascists, communists, socialists, and members of the co-operative movement, to mention some of the more important programs—all have their solutions to our problems. We shall make no attempt to set forth the assumptions, principles, and practices of these social philosophies. There is considerable doubt, however, whether the future will conform to any single pattern. The future may have to grow out of the present in ways that cannot always be predicted, although a considerable degree of human control may be possible.

The capitalistic order, which stresses the concepts of free enterprise, competition, profit motive, and private property, has made contributions to civilization. It is not all evil, nor is it all good. It has given us mass production and a high degree of technological efficiency. Considerable cultural enrichment has resulted as a by-product. Individualism may have been the best means of conquering the new continent. On the other hand, it appears today that certain features of it are obsolete and will have to go. Society can no longer tolerate the effects of ruthless competition and an uncurbed profit motive. The appeal to self-interest will need to be replaced by motives that are more social and ethical. The financial and industrial systems of our day are changing rapidly. Whereas the old economy was dominated by small business units, "free" competition, flexible prices, and equality in bargaining power, the newer economy is dominated by large corporations, administrative competition, inflexible prices in many commodities, and inequality in bargaining power. Ware and Means, after setting forth these contrasts, suggest that under the new conditions the profit motive drives the officials of corporations "to make decisions which tend to wreck the economic machine." [8] While many capitalists are honorable and public spirited men, too many take the attitude, "soak the public" and "make your pile"; then "hang on and dodge the government." Capitalism is being tried both on the basis of its ability to care for the population, and for its behavior in the court of morals.

Fascism has been mentioned from time to time in our discussions. Fascism substitutes the rule of force for the principles of law and morals. Naked self-assertion and the drive for domination over others represent the denial of ethics. The "get-power-quick" racket is no better than the "get-money-quick" racket. Fascism, as we have seen, appears to be at war with the free, self-disciplined personality, the Christian ethics, and a rational order of society. The chief doctrines and attitudes represented by fascism stand in sharp opposition to the marks of a mature morality which we have considered. Totalitarianism is false and dangerous. No institution ought to be an end in and of itself.

In actual practice, communism in Russia has exhibited

many of the outward features that we find in fascism. For example, we find a ruthless dictatorship, a denial of liberty to unsympathetic groups, and an emphasis upon revolution and force as methods. These tactics, however, are considered as means rather than accepted as ideal ends. So far as theory is concerned, communism has little in common with fascism, as we pointed out in chapter two. There is in communism a passion for social justice, and a drive to establish the brotherhood of man in a society where liberty, democracy, and an equality of abundance will prevail. Communism embraces some ends that are in harmony with the principles of a mature morality and some elements that appear to be a denial of such a morality.

Socialism is a tendency rather than a strictly definable body of doctrine, and there are many types or varieties of socialists. Socialists believe that the surplus arising from the economic system and from improvements should go for the common welfare and not to any single individual or group; also that society can be so organized and controlled that all persons can be assured of the means of a good life. In so far as they stand for a greater degree of co-operation, for democratic methods, and oppose the exploitation of man by man, they are to be commended. The chief danger in socialism would seem to be the possibility of too great a control over life thus delaying social progress, and a danger of bureaucracy in government. If these dangers are not real, as the socialists claim, there would be little objection to the program of the socialists. The trend toward increasing social regulation of industrial and business activities appeared long before the New Deal and is likely to continue.

The Consumer Co-operative Movement attempts to satisfy both the practical and the idealistic needs of man. While raising the standard of living it seeks to develop social-mindedness and democratic living. It conducts business without profit, or more strictly by distributing the surplus to the consumers who use the services. The emphasis is upon persons and human values rather than upon profits and property. It organizes society on a voluntary non-political basis in which persons, not shares of stock, vote. Probably the strongest arguments for the co-operative movement are ethical, since each person succeeds in proportion as everyone else succeeds. No one benefits from dishonesty or poor quality of merchandise. The co-operative movement has received considerable support from religious leaders. In the past, they have felt that they have been trying to make a code of ethics fit an unethical social and economic order of society. In the outlook of the co-operative movement, they found a technique that seemed to them to square with the ethics they were endeavoring to teach. They found it hard to teach a gospel of love and fellowship in an economic order founded so largely on the principle of every man for himself.

Many persons desire to face the problems of modern society without complete commitment to any one program or type of social philosophy. They see the need, however, of the further extension or application of the principles of a mature Christian morality to our group relationships. Most men recognize that killing, injuring, stealing, lying, and the like, are immoral acts. If I steal your pocketbook or lie to you, the act is condemned. Yet where our great-grandfathers knew a comparatively few, simple ways of killing, injuring, stealing, and lying, there are today hundreds of new ways of doing these things of which they knew nothing. Some of the new ways are indirect, and have not as yet come under our condemnation. Technological development has outstripped the evolution of morality. I can kill or injure by means of the defective construction of bridges and buildings, by food adulteration, by quack doctoring, and by stirring up international hatred. To gain a monopoly and to raise the price of milk will affect milk consumption and the infant mortality rates will rise. I can steal by means of "watered stock" and the gaining of a franchise through "pull." I can lie by means of advertising, propaganda, and biased journalism.

How to bring organizations to regulate their acts by the principles of a mature morality is one of the difficult problems of our time. Directors and officials of such institutions as corporations and states must be made to feel a personal sense of responsibility for acts performed by the organizations of which they are a part. We must think of corporations, for example, as groups of individuals and hold the individuals, as well as the corporations, morally and legally responsible for anti-social behavior. Some of the great evils of our day are caused by men who are perhaps honest and kind in their personal relations, but who lack the moral vision and the knowledge to foresee the ill effects of their corporate acts. Wrongdoing tends to change its form with changes in the social order. Modern men, while sensitive to the traditional forms of wrongdoing, do not always recognize the immoral acts made possible by their newer ways of living.

The Delaware Conference, under the auspices of the Commission on a Just and Durable Peace of the Federal Council of Churches, went on record as follows: "We believe that moral law, no less than physical law, undergirds our world. There is a moral order which is fundamental and eternal, and which is relevant to the corporate life of men and the ordering of human society. If mankind is to escape chaos and recurrent war, social and political institutions must be brought into conformity with this moral order."

As stated in a previous section of this chapter, the immediate future is likely to see the development of a society in which areas of private initiative and enterprise will be bounded by areas of social ownership and control and by developing areas under voluntary co-operative groups. The achievement of a good society is a long, slow task. The only justification for any social, economic, or political institution is that it promotes human welfare on a broad basis more adequately than can any other institution that might be substituted for it. Social organization alone will not solve all our problems. We need good men who are intelligent and who live in a just society.

CHAPTER VIII

THE CRISIS AND OUR RESPONSIBILITY

IN THE FIRST CHAPTER, we pointed out that we live in an age of uncertainty and confusion in which many of the things that men desire and love seem to be threatened with destruction. Problems have been increasing and there is a precariousness about the values of life including a widespread fear that civilization itself may be in a period of decline. Our study has carried us through a consideration of the basis and nature of moral ideals and their relation to religion and to human welfare in general.

Clearly we face a crisis that is deeper and more serious than most people realize. The existence of civilization hangs in the balance. The mere compulsion of tradition and the weight of custom have lost their force. Mankind is now engaged in one of its rare moods of shifting its outlook and its basic assumptions. Such periods occur only infrequently in human history. Men of good will and intelligence face the task of furnishing a vision of the world and an integrating ideal without which society will remain in confusion and conflict. We must produce a great age, one more in harmony with human aspirations, or see the collapse and loss of many of the gains of the past. Great decisions are being made, and will be made in our time. They will affect the course of history for years to come.

We have used the term "crisis" in referring to the present stirring period in history. A friend from China tells me that the Chinese word for "crisis" is a double word meaning "danger" and "opportunity." A crisis is a "dangerous opportunity." The Greek word (κρίσις) implies a judging or judgment, and the idea of a decision. In modern medical language a "crisis" means the turning-point of a disease. When this occurs it will become clear whether the patient will have sufficient strength to throw off the disease or whether he will be overcome by it. We call the present period of rapid change or cultural transition a crisis, because it has reached a stage in its development where the very existence of our civilization hangs in the balance. The world is likely to be pitched to a new high or a new low in the decades just ahead. Men must decide whether they are to go this way or that and what values are to be retained. It is a period of danger, of opportunity, and of decision.

Interpretations of the Crisis

Before considering further the nature of the period in which we live, let us consider some of the explanations that are current today. Of the many and various explanations, let us briefly consider five lines of interpretation without explaining them in much detail. There is first the view that the crisis is the result of the efforts of a few evil men, a group of political gangsters or greedy racketeers, who "muscled in," so to speak, and who were able by cunning trickery and clever propaganda to deceive the unsuspecting masses in certain countries. These national and international racketeers would first create a danger and stimulate fear, then go to the person or group or nation involved and offer "protection" against the danger. A handsome price or reward was always demanded. The "get-power-quick" racket, it is claimed, is not much different from the "get-money-quick" racket which we have witnessed in many cities, except that it is on a vaster scale with higher stakes. According to this rather popular interpretation, if we could just get rid of men like Hitler and Mussolini, everything would be all right again.

A second approach is to view the crisis as the result of some temporary maladjustment or disorder in the machinery or organization of society. Such things as the failure to return her former colonies to Germany, the breakdown of the League of Nations, excessively high tariffs, or the manipulation of the currency, may be stressed. Some other persons seem to believe that the one thing wrong with the world is the treaty of Versailles. Such interpretations may stress economic or political factors, or some combination of them. According to these interpretations if we could get the right laws or make the proper adjustments in our political and economic machinery we might have clear sailing ahead.

Closely allied to the above interpretation is a third which interprets the turmoil of our age as the disturbances accompanying the last and violent stage of capitalism. Capitalism, it is said, is in its death struggle. The fascists came to power because in the last resort the privileged groups in the capitalist countries preferred capitalism to democracy. When the rise of democracy, and its spread among the masses, threatened to reduce the power, the control, and the privileges of the wealthy groups they chose to retain their privileges and to scuttle democracy. Totalitarianism was promoted as a counter movement to crush the insurgency of the people. It has been referred to as an attempt by political means to fix the economic situation at a point where "maximum security of existing property rights can be maintained." Various writers, including Harold Laski, the outstanding political scientist of London, take this interpretation. It is definitely Marxian in its outlook.

A fourth interpretation is that the crisis is the result of a long, slowly developing, but deep-rooted tradition of absolutism, authoritarianism, and of state worship, that has just come to the surface during recent years. According to this view, Mussolini and Hitler are merely the popularizers of doctrines which originated centuries ago and which sought the elevation of the state and the subordination of the individual. A recent book by McGovern entitled *From Luther to Hitler* explains and traces the rise of this tradition and ideology which rejects freedom, democracy, and the liberal movement, which elevates the state and the race, and which looks toward dictatorial control.

Finally, there are those who claim that explanations like the above, while they cannot be ignored completely, are too superficial. We are in the midst of a world revolution which is affecting the very foundations of our society. This global war is merely the more violent phase of great basic changes which are taking place. We are witnessing the breakdown of a social order which has dominated Western civilization for some centuries. Earlier revolutions in history, like the American and French revolutions, were local or national in scope, because of limited contact and communication. Today we are in the midst of a revolution which is world wide due to the fact that our communications and contacts are world wide.

Which one of these interpretations is most accurate? Of course they overlap to some extent and each may contain some truth. To interpret the crisis as the result of the effort of a few evil men is exceedingly superficial. They have been evil enough, even devilish or diabolical, and they have aggravated the situation tremendously and made it more violent than it might have been. They are, however, products rather than causes of the crisis. We certainly need changes and reorganization in our political, economic, and social orders, but these interpretations singly or in combination do not go deep enough and are too superficial. To overcome the disorders of our age more than tinkering with machinery is needed. Even economic planning and social engineering, though necessary in a machine age, are merely techniques which in themselves possess no saving grace. We can plan ourselves into barbarism as well as into social security.

While the capitalists have frequently turned freedom into license and have been guilty of exploitation, this explanation alone is not enough. While some capitalists aided the rise of fascism many others opposed it. Whether and to what extent capitalism will be able to survive the needed changes in society is an open question. Certainly, if it survives, it will be greatly modified and changed. To interpret the crisis as the result of a tradition of absolutism and state worship does not tell us why so many persons have felt the need of looking to the state for security.

I am inclined to believe that the fifth interpretation is the most accurate one. We are facing a revolution which is moral, intellectual, and spiritual, as well as political and economic. The crisis of our times is a crisis involving man's loyalty and faith. It is caused by a world-wide revolt against civilization as well as by a disintegration of that civilization. People are frustrated by interpretations of life which take all meaning and significance from it, by economic institutions which result in poverty and insecurity in the midst of plenty, and by antiquated political organizations and barriers which lead to conflict. Personal, political, and economic immorality have combined to produce our international immorality and anarchy. The war is but the outward manifestation of a serious moral and spiritual impoverishment.

Those who think that the present conflict is "just another war" are deluding themselves. In the present war there are basic ideological differences. As we have seen, fascism and democracy, and fascism and the ideals upon which Western civilization have been built, represent two diametrically opposed ways of life. Due to the stage of social and technological evolution which we have reached, the war is total in that it affects all persons and all areas of life. It is psychological, and social, as well as military in the traditional sense. There is a spirit of collectivism, as well as a spirit of brutality, not in evidence in recent wars. This war, again, cuts across national boundaries. While there have always been some traitors, this is the first war in which the "fifth column" has assumed major proportions. One reason why the fascist countries so nearly won the war in 1940 was because the leaders in the democratic nations failed to understand it. Many of those leaders are beginning to understand it today and to realize that we cannot go back to the nineteenth century; nor to the decade of the twenties; no, not even to 1939. Those who think we can are living in a world of unreality. To attempt the preservation of things as they are, in a world of injustice, is as immoral as it is impossible. We are in a revolutionary period and we need to understand the forces involved.

Not only the statesmen and politicians, but the moral and religious leaders have been divided and confused. Some of them seemed to think that they could save the nation by talking about the sinfulness of war, working for disarmament, and keeping the United States strictly neutral. Many of them never insisted that their country identify itself with the Permanent Court of International Jusice, the League of Nations, and other instruments for the establishment of world order. While excellent pronouncements were made by groups of Christians at such conferences as Oxford, Edinburgh, Geneva, and Madras, and while Christians, in theory, regarded themselves as members of one all-inclusive family under the Fatherhood of God, in actual practice many of them seemed to forget that they were citizens of the world. The churches as a whole did not seriously challenge the world anarchy and immorality.

Some Next Steps

Granting that war itself is one of the greatest of evils which must be eliminated, I believe that the present war must be brought to a successful conclusion and that we ought to do all in our power to defeat the axis powers. We must have a world in which we are free to think, to plan, and to work for a better world. Unless the fascist leadership is eliminated and the fascist countries defeated, there is little point in our talking about the kind of world we want after the war. Everything will be settled for us. We have taken our freedom, our rights, our way of life, and our spiritual heritage so much for granted that it is hard for us to appreciate what their loss would mean. We shall have to make sacrifices in order to retain our heritage as free moral human beings. But let us not delude ourselves. The crisis will not be over when the war is won. We shall have then only the opportunity to face our problems and to endeavor to solve them. Military victory is only the first step.

In working to defeat the axis nations and to eliminate their present leadership, let us not come to hate peoples, nations, or races. Hatred tends to destroy the hater as well as the hated. Emotions of hatred, once strongly developed, are likely to continue and to express themselves in lynchings, race riots, labor disturbances, and other disorders. We shall have enough unfortunate results of this tragic war without having deep, pent-up, destructive hatreds. If we resent and oppose injustices and tyranny, our resentment will go when those things are eliminated. If we hate peoples that hatred is likely to continue indefinitely. The basis for wholesome morale is not hatred, but rather confidence in the ideals and values underlying our free way of life, fear that this way of life may be lost, and faith in the possibility of a better world.

In the first World War, 1914-1918, we won the war and lost the peace. This time we must win both the war and the peace. Otherwise our children will be forced to face a third and more hideous war. It is possible for us and our children to live in a better world than any race of men have yet seen, a world without war and poverty. I say it is possible, but there is no certainty. We may live in a much worse world than any recent generations have known.

Leaders in all walks of American life ought to be studying carefully such documents as "The Atlantic Charter," the reports of the Commission to Study the Organization of Peace of which Dr. James T. Shotwell is chairman, and the reports of the Commission to Study the Basis of a Just and Durable Peace of the Federal Council of the Churches of Christ in America. To discuss the particular proposals which are being made for a just and enduring peace would carry us beyond the scope of this book. The following one-hundred word statement [1] is an unofficial summary of the findings of the Delaware Conference held under the auspices of the Federal Council of Churches:

As Christians we seek:

1. A just and durable peace, founded on world-wide brotherhood.
2. No hatred or revenge.
3. Full American co-operation to feed, heal and rebuild the shattered world.
4. Prevention of aggressive wars by a strong, just and democratic world commonwealth of nations.
5. Full membership by America in this world government.

6. Mutual abandonment of aggressive armaments by all nations.
7. Elimination of trade barriers.
8. Other measures to raise standards of living in all nations.
9. International protection of the rights of colonies and of hitherto subject peoples.
10. Safeguarding the rights and liberties of Jews, Negroes and all other minorities.

If we are to win the peace and to eliminate the causes of war, it is necessary to recognize clearly the causes of the war and the crisis. Nothing but ignorance or hypocrisy can lead us to place all the blame upon any small group of men or upon one or two nations. The moral guilt is shared by the leaders and the peoples of all nations. The crisis has been caused by the pagan secularism which was rampant all over the world, expressing itself in a rabid nationalism, in power politics, and in economic imperialism. Fascism is only the most hideous and offensive form of it. The war has been going on, under cover, for decades. Walter W. Van Kirk says that it is "childish to suppose that wars start with shooting," and he suggests that the Second World War began the very hour when the First World War was ended. For some years it continued as a "Battle for Reparations." The German people, after financial ruin and years of bitterness began to look for a deliverer, and Hitler was the answer. Then followed the "Battle of Trade Discrimination" of which the Fordney-McCumber tariff of 1921 and the Smoot-Hawley tariff of 1930 were incidents. This battle was followed by depression and more despair. The "Battle of Raw Materials," with its trade cartels, monopolies, and quota systems, followed. This battle left great food surpluses in some nations and near starvation in others. A shooting war was the inevitable result of this cruel struggle for privilege and gain. Dr. Van Kirk says:

"Along with other nations the United States must accept its full share of responsibility for Hitler. We refused to join the League of Nations. We refused to join the World Court. We withdrew from the World Economic Conference. We separated ourselves from the rest of the world. We closed our eyes. We closed our ears. We closed our minds. We closed our hearts. We did everything but close our mouths. And from that day until the outbreak of the Second World War we preached international morality for others and practiced international anarchy for ourselves." [2]

In many respects the war is a Judgment of God upon us as well as upon the nations of the world. The world is still a moral order and meaningful. The crisis is due to no accident or temporary storm; it is a natural growth from the seeds of destruction which the nations have been sowing. Men cannot play fast and loose with moral laws and not reap the whirlwind. As Maude Royden is quoted as saying: "If this war had not occurred, I would have found it hard to believe in God." There is a moral order in the universe and men have been trying to ignore it, but they cannot do so for long. Every society rests upon some moral and spiritual foundations which can be discovered in the ideas, ideals, motives, values, and loyalties of its members. As Herbert Agar has well said, "We are at war primarily because of the sickness of our civilization that made all these events necessary. . . . In a world in which 'anything goes' everything will soon be gone." [3]

The crisis will not be over until men come to feel, individually and collectively, responsible for molding their domestic and international relations in harmony with the Christian ethics or the demands of a mature morality. The eras of "every man for himself" and of isolation are over. As human beings we shall either live together or we shall die together. Neither statism, nor racialism, nor regionalism will do. We must have a world community of international law and some form of world government. The peoples of the world must live together and work together in the future. Technological developments, including modern means of transportation and communication, have made that imperative. This "togetherness" necessitates co-operation, sharing, order, organization. The only alternative to this is world anarchy.

What Can We Do?

There is a widespread feeling that something ought to be done, that we ought to produce a great age out of the turmoil of the present. Young persons who are alert are especially likely to ask, "What can we do about it?" The question may take the form of "What can one person do?" It may be asked with a shrug of the shoulders, or with an attitude that means, "There isn't much we can do." There are at least four reactions that men have regarding their responsibility, or lack of it, for the problems and the violence of our age. First, there are a few who see the evils of our time and who declare that there is no meaning or rational justification for life. They deny that any responsibility falls upon them. They may give way to cynicism or despair. Some are bitter that life has given them problems instead of uninterrupted happiness. A character in a recent play is quoted as saying, "What can I say? I've said it all. Nothing matters but happiness. Get your share. Life's a racket. Loyalty's a joke. We've debunked everything but lust." [4]

Second, there are those who would like to do something, but who feel that the task is too great to face. Some years ago, according to reports, a student came from the little country of Iraq, in the Near East, to study at one of the large American universities. Soon after his arrival he was taken on a tour around and through the university by an American. They visited, among other buildings, the library where they walked through tier upon tier of books in the library stacks. The American thought that the lad would be thrilled and delighted with the opportunity before him, but to his great surprise the foreign student was discouraged and said that he thought he would return to his native land and continue his studies there. Then the American discovered the reason for his reaction. In Iraq there are from a thousand to two thousand books, and an educated man can expect to read and become familiar with all these books. But hundreds of thousands of books—that was simply impossible. As they view the complex problems facing the world today, some modern Americans have a somewhat similar reaction. They would like to do something but they find it hard to move into effective action. Like some of the refugees on the roads in front of the German blitzkrieg in Europe, they become weary and wait to see what will happen.

Third, there are those who try to turn away and forget. In one form or another their reaction is one of escape. The constitutionally weaker persons may find escape in the mental diseases. They live in a world of unreality and build their castles there. Others turn to alcohol which temporarily deadens the upper centers. A few resort to suicide. Some turn off the radio and get relief in a whirl of social activities. Some young people live a rather happy animal existence, living mainly for the next date, the next dance, or the next meal. There are numerous ways of shutting oneself off from the world.

Fourth, there are the more penetrating and courageous persons who know the worst and yet realize that no situation is so bad that men of intelligence and good will cannot do something about it. They have a grim determination to get the facts, to face up to the whole situation, and to see it through. They want to eliminate the evil and to use the present good as the basis for building something better. These persons usually have more curiosity and persistency. If they go far enough they usually discover that there is much that makes life worth living. These persons are more mature in their reactions. They are more responsive and more responsible. They are men and women of stronger moral fibre. If civilization is to be saved, it will be by members of this latter group.

Some of the great tasks of the world have been carried out, or at least initiated, by one man or one woman. Nearly one hundred years ago in the Crimean War, men were dying at the rate of forty-two to one hundred in the army hospitals. Florence Nightingale went to the Crimea and within a few months the death rate of soldiers in the hospitals she supervised had dropped to two in a hundred patients. During this time her society friends in London were saying, "What can a woman do?" Baden Powell saw boys in his city becoming delinquent at a rapid rate. What could one man do? He noticed how their desire for play, their love of adventure, and even their delinquent acts could be converted into the means for making useful men and building strong character. Soon the Boy Scout movement was building up self-control, courage, loyalty, and a sense of responsibility to society. The American Red Cross is connected with the name of Clara Barton and prison reform with that of John Howard. A few years ago, *Reader's Digest* carried a series of articles called "Honorable Mention." Month after month it listed cases or incidents of notable achievements for human welfare initiated by single individuals or by small groups.

Some of the individuals, mentioned above, organized groups to help in carrying out their purpose. To be most effective as individuals we need to combine and co-operate with our fellows, that is, to form groups for this or that purpose. This does not mean that we shall be lost in the crowd, or that we have to suppress our individuality. It means that we must co-operate with others and broaden our sympathies. Even those with evil intent usually realize the need of operating in groups. Most criminals operate in gangs. There are political machines and pressure groups of all kinds. Too frequently the "good" man thinks that his individual goodness is all that is necessary. The extreme individualist will prefer to go his own way, thinking that his individual intelligence and upright life are all that is needed. This is quite erroneous as there are many things men can do together which they cannot do separately. To carry out social and political aims we need to work with other persons who are like-minded, or at least who have similar interests. To prevent unemployment, poverty, economic depressions, political corruption, and war, we need to join groups and to act with others.

We can have individual worship which is good, but if our worship is to mean much and if our religious efforts are to be effective in the community, we need to join with others in a church. We can have our own opinions, but if they are to be most effective we need to join with others in discussion. In this way we get new ideas and our views may be modified and extended. We need protection in life from numerous hazards and losses. As we join with others in insurance groups and each individual bears small but regular burdens, each gains more adequate protection than he could get alone. We want to help others who are in distress, but our opportunities and power to do so may be very limited. We may even do more harm than good if we do not know the circumstances and causes. As we join each other, in giving to such organizations as the Community Chest, our help may be widely extended. As business and professional men we want to

eliminate evils and to establish higher standards in our chosen
fields, we can do these most effectively as we work through
our trade and professional organizations. To cope with problems of world order we shall need trans-national or international organizations. Part of the art of life consists in knowing
when and how to use available organizations and instrumentalities to forward the purposes of life. When adequate instruments are not available we have to create new ones.

The very fact that a man is living in society, partaking of
its activity, buying and selling, working and playing, approv-
ing and disapproving, loving and hating, means that his life
is counting one way or another. He cannot escape personal
and social responsibility. If he faces a problem and refuses to
decide, time decides the issue for him. Regardless of their
station in life there are some things that all men of goodwill
and a degree of intelligence can do. Let us consider a few
of these things.

First, each person can study and do a little more thinking
for himself. He can read the "signs of the times" and help
discover the causes of confusion and decay. He can help to
check the modern "retreat from reason." He can be a center
of information and, in the better sense, of agitation for the
values that are most worthwhile. He can resist the tendency
to settle issues by means of emotion, prejudice, propaganda,
and violence.

Thinking is stimulated when there are doubt, perplexity,
and problems to face. If that is true, then the present period
ought to stir men to do some really creative thinking. As one
editor, writing during the recent depression, said, "After all,
are we not fortunate to live in the age of unsettlement? The
times of certainty are also the times of stagnation. When we
know what to think, we cease to think. When conditions of
life are fixed, we merely tramp the treadmill in them. The

great periods are the new ones, when, because everything is undone, everything has to be done. . . .

". . . Our misfortune is not that we are thrust into a time when thinking must be done, but that we do not do it. It was a thousand years after the Roman Empire fell before men realized that they were no longer living in it. Many of us still imagine that we are living in the world that died forever on August 1, 1914. Recent events are shaking us out of that illusion. The process is painful, but it may be salutary. It challenges us to think new thoughts. The first and hardest step in that process is to unthink the old ones. Or, perhaps, for some of us, to think at all. This is no time for the slothful." [5]

If we are to improve our thinking we must start with a genuine desire to face facts and to be significantly informed. Flexibility of mind is essential, as is a tolerant attitude that wants to face facts and is willing to be convinced by evidence. We shall also need to exercise vigilance in an effort to keep the sources of our information free from manipulation and propaganda. The future of the world depends, in considerable part, on the habit of thinking, or forming opinions on evidence, rather than upon blind impulse, stereotypes, or upon mere tradition.

Second, after we have gained information and knowledge, we must learn to apply the results of our study and thinking more fully than we have in the past. As a nation of specialists, we have applied our technical knowledge to our separate fields, but as specialists we have assumed little or no responsibility for human affairs and our social relationships. Here we have fallen down woefully. The main problem of our society is not so much a lack of study and research but this dangerous separation of science and research from human values and loyalties. The specialists have taken refuge behind the postulates of "objectivity," "impersonality," and dispassionate research. Specialization and departmentalization have increased in all fields until we tend to see life in fragments or in parts and to lose our sense of its unity, its meaning, and its wholeness. To assume that we add to human understanding by disconnected additions of factual knowledge on many separate subjects, without attempting to determine the relation of one field to another, is probably fallacious. No intelligent person would propose that we stop gathering facts and data, but only that we make a more valuable use of the data we have already collected.

The natural scientists have felt that their interests and desires must not enter into their research, and the social scientists have tended to follow their lead. But if social science is the study of man and of human society, and if man is a feeling as well as a thinking being, the social scientist should not treat man as if he were functioning merely on the physical level. The social scientist ought to look to philosophy, art, and religion to furnish some of the principles by which he studies man's relation to man.

Specialization is of tremendous value and ought not to be hindered. There is, however, the probability that the attitude of detachment has gone too far. A university president in a large city remarked in my presence a few years ago that if he had some project of human welfare which he wished to bring before the public, the last group to which he would think of going, if he were in search of assistance, would be the university club of the city. They were a group of specialists with little sense of community responsibility. A teacher in sociology, when asked a question about some social problem facing society, replied, "I am not interested in betterment. I am a scientist interested in discovering and describing facts." That attitude can be understood better on the basis of the late nineteenth-century assumption of inevitable progress. Assuming that the race was moving upward all the specialist had to do was to put new facts and new tools in man's hands and that would accelerate the rate of progress. Now, we are beginning to see the folly of that approach. Progress is possible, but not inevitable at any one period of history. Science and technical skill may be used by vicious men to destroy civilization as well as by men of goodwill to promote human welfare.

The effort to look upon human action with the same ethical neutrality with which we view an equation in arithmetic is understandable, but the problems of human values are inescapable and we ought to face them. Are we to leave the application of new knowledge to the demagogue or the rabble rouser? Should our vast army of specialists not feel as responsible for the application of knowledge as for its acquisition? While each person ought to learn to do some particular thing, which is worth doing, and to do it well, he ought also to see its relation to society as a whole and to human values. The important thing is not mere knowledge and education, but the kind of education. One can teach a dog to kill sheep or to protect sheep. We need a new kind of education that stresses the motives that are social and one which, like adult education, will continue throughout life. Of equal importance with the acquisition of "facts" is the ability to think and to evaluate things.

Specialists, including the vast army of scientists and research workers, are often progressives or even radicals in their own special fields, but tend to be conservatives or reactionaries in nearly everything else. This is especially true regarding their attitude toward human or social relationships and problems. This attitude may enable them to avoid numerous controversies with the public, but it also contributes to the moral and cultural lag of our times. In a revolutionary period and crisis, such as we face, this attitude may be disastrous. The public outlook upon moral and social questions is not keeping pace with the progress of science and mechanical invention. Men dedicated to the use of scientific method, experimentation, and reflective thinking in their own fields contribute to obscurantism in other fields.

Third, we can keep our ideals alive and growing. We can refuse to give up our hope and our faith in a better world. Our ideals keep before us the direction in which we ought to be moving. They are the growing points of our experience, and as we tend to reach them, they should grow and expand too. There is nothing like a devotion to something higher and better than present actualities to give life meaning and zest.

Man lives in two worlds at the same time. He lives in a present, tangible, physical world of sense-perception, and in an emerging, unseen world of ideals, values, and ends. The will to live is expressed at first on the physical level. Man must have food, clothing, shelter, and self-preservation. In man, however, there is not only the will to live, there is also the will to live *well*. Man is not satisfied with what *is*. He seeks for something better and higher. He seeks for the meaning of his life, and for understanding and fellowship with the more ultimate elements upon which his life depends. Religion and morality find their meaning in man's response and attempt to integrate these two worlds. Man's aspirations and ideals are his partly conscious realization of his own inherent possibilities. Man wants to know if goodness, truth, and beauty are among the enduring elements of the universe, and he wants to unify the two worlds.

Undoubtedly great masses of people have lost their ideals or have become weary in attempting to reach them. They may have decided to live exclusively on the lower level and "to eat, drink, and be merry," or they may merely lack any great cause for which to live. This is especially true of many young people. After considerable contact with young people while on the university preaching mission, E. Stanley Jones says: "I came to America to convert and soon found myself converted. First, I was converted to American youth. I expected to find a blasé, fed-up, sophisticated group of young people, but instead I found the finest raw human material that this country has ever produced—frank, upstanding, prepared, but confused, and, when you can get to it, wistful and hungry. They are far finer and more open than the students of ten years ago. But one thing they do not have—they have no cause. They are all dressed up and do not know where to go. Nothing grips them supremely. And the tragedy is that they do not see it.

"One youth objected in these words when I said they did not have a cause: 'But we do have a cause; we want to succeed.' Personal success is the only gripping thing on the campus. And the tragedy is that he thought that a cause. But that confusion has been bequeathed by the older generation. Personal success in terms of money accumulation and power is the best that an economic and social order such as ours can give to youth. Did anything ever so reveal its own bankruptcy?" [6]

A member of the present student generation expresses very well the problem of many young people and the struggle to retain their ideals. "Mine is a disillusioned generation. From father and mother, from teacher and preacher, in poem and story, we have heard through all our childhood all the tragic inconsistencies of war. We have learned to hate the beating drums and the uniform. We have been taught to take the

Germans as individuals, not as 'Kaiserites.' We have learned to respect the Scandinavians and the Swiss for their peaceful attitude in the World War.

"Now we are twenty-one. All our childhood lessons and loyalties must be forgotten. Those who taught us these lessons have changed their attitudes on the grounds of a national crisis. War has become a necessity, an honorable means to defend an honorable cause. We must clothe ourselves in the hated uniform and learn to march to the unloved beat of the drum. Our creed is no longer 'peace' but 'all-out aid to Britain.' The Germans have become 'Hitlerites' who must be defeated at any cost. The Scandinavians are reprimanded as slow and unprepared because they fell before the invader. Some of us are making the change willingly; others are more persistent in their childhood faiths.

"All of us are disillusioned. We cling to our ideals, but we face the hated realities of compulsory military training and a promise of war, with perhaps the accent on death. Few of us can learn to support a war earnestly against a twenty year habit. We hope for life, and a saner world after the war. Perhaps a lovelier world will take shape out of the chaos, and we must help to mold it. All we can do is live, and live hopefully and courageously and keep our faith in a better world to be." [7]

We can strive to keep our own ideals alive and also help other persons to retain theirs. Members of the older generations can admit the failure of their generations to create a more ideal world and encourage the coming generation to keep "faith in a better world to be." Ideals are tremendous forces in the lives of men and women. Even powerful drives like hunger and sex may be denied expression in the interest of some ideal. Different civilizations have been the expression of different ideals of life. We can literally change men and social trends by changing the ideas and ideals to which men give their loyalty.

If our ideals are to become actualities we need to support movements that point in the direction of our ideals even though they are not perfect. This is the melioristic attitude which has been mentioned already. Progress is made by a little gain here and a little advance there, not by standing still. Each person needs to ask himself the question: "What kind of a world do I wish to see emerge after the present crisis or conflict?" In order to keep alive to the possibilities and the directions in which we want the world to move, Dr. H. A. Overstreet [8] suggests that every individual keep "A Notebook of Tomorrow" in which he jots down suggestions regarding what he thinks the world of tomorrow ought to be. Defects of the present system and possible improvements could be recorded. Dr. Overstreet suggests that if the notebook is blank after six months, a man should turn his critical gaze inward upon himself. Quite apart from such proposals, we can make our influence felt in many ways. We can oppose sex discrimination, racial bigotry and prejudice, corruption, and injustice wherever we find them. We can help to promote equality of opportunity, the spread of knowledge, higher living standards, cleaner politics, and social justice in general.

This is no time for discouragement and despair. Victory frequently builds upon apparent defeat. If it is true that "something is brewing when things go wrong," the present may be laden with great potentialities. Once when the Liberal cause was defeated in England, the leader, Mr. Gladstone, is said to have risen undaunted in Parliament and said, "I appeal to time." In a similar situation when his reforms were meeting vigorous opposition, John Bright is said to have remarked, "If we can't win as fast as we wish, we know that our opponents can't win in the long run at all."

The society of tomorrow must be built slowly and continuously as we meet the issues of life and from materials which are available. There is an interesting account of the building of the Grand Central Station in New York City. Once there was on that site an obsolete and inadequate structure. While keeping the older station operating and the trains running on schedule, men tunnelled into the rock beneath, opened up fifty new tracks on two levels and completed the new station without loss and delay. Something like this must be done in our society. An early president of Antioch College is quoted as saying, "Be ashamed to die until you have won some victory for humanity." At least we have the responsibility to see that progress is no slower than it need be. We can help or hinder the struggle toward a better world. The chief danger is that we fail to understand the revolution through which we are passing, and to act intelligently toward it.

Grounds For Encouragement

Earlier in the chapter we referred to those more penetrating and courageous persons who face all the facts and know the worst regarding the world in which they live, and yet who are resolved to build a better world. They want this better world for themselves and others but, if not for themselves, at least for their children and for posterity. There are three things that should offer much encouragement to this group. With these we shall bring our discussion to a close.

The first is that life and the future are not fixed or completely determined or inevitable as some would have us believe. The economic and other deterministic interpretations of history, popular in recent years, have blinded us to the significance of the ethical and social attitudes of peoples. The specialists of our age have concentrated upon things and animals rather than upon men. When they have turned their attention to men they have tended to study those aspects of human beings which belong to the world of things and the world of animals. Too frequently they have overlooked man as a moral being who gains more and more freedom as he increases in knowledge, intelligence, or understanding. All persons and all peoples simply do not react in the same way to what are essentially the same material conditions. The response depends to a considerable extent upon the ideas and the ideals which are ingrained in the thinking and conduct of the people. The economic and material conditions may provide the stimulus, but they do not wholly determine the response.

History is made very largely by those who make up their minds, providing they make them up with sufficient unity, intelligence, and courage. History is a history of human beings and not just an account of the behavior of animals and of economic forces. Men live at that point where law and freedom are somehow joined. If there were only law there would be no choice and no human achievements. If there were only freedom there would be continuous confusion and anarchy. Civilization is the result of human intelligence and good will choosing among possible alternatives in the light of principles tested by the experience of the race. Within certain limits men can choose their destiny and their future.

To scan the long period of human progress in the past should give us courage and faith for the future. We have a rich heritage in the fields of art, science, philosophy, and religion. We have already eliminated many of the former enemies of mankind, and we have available the resources for building a higher civilization than any race of men have ever known. Due to modern knowledge and the means of discovering trends and remedies, we have a greater possibility of conscious choice and control than ever before. We have the possibility, *if* we have the insight, the courage, and the will to do so.

A second reason for encouragement is that a minority, small groups, sometimes unique persons, can generate the creative forces to revitalize and to redeem a society. Perhaps it would be more correct to say that they become the channels through which creative forces act upon society. A small group of persons with vision, and devotion to the will of God as they see it, can set the pace and attract the less creative and less sensitive majority. Students of Hebrew history will be familiar with the conception of the "Remnant," a small minority of true believers, in whom the hope of the nation rested. The prophets, Isaiah, Jeremiah, and Ezekiel, arose at times of national crises and preached the doctrine of the survival of the Remnant. Sometimes the Remnant was the small, true "Israel" which was to mediate salvation to the larger or political Israel whose waywardness was leading to ruin. At other times Judaism itself seemed to be the Remnant to bring life to all the nations. Christianity arose out of small beginnings to change the course of history. It began with a few fishermen and others who kept company with Jesus and who learned a new way of life. Small groups within the Christian communion have continuously brought new life and vitality to the larger movement.

Writers in the field of the philosophy of history, like Toynbee, have also called our attention to the power of small, alert, and creative groups in all periods of history.[9] These groups often give new life to society and check the forces of decay. When a "Creative Minority degenerates into a mere Dominant Minority" which attempts to retain its privileged position by other means than merit, society ceases to follow, and social confusion begins. The "floating vote" is given to the Creative Minority, according to Toynbee.

Today, if enough persons can be found who revolt against the materialistic secularism, the spirit of selfish acquisitiveness, the spirit of thoughtlessness, and against prejudice and bigotry, they may lead toward a new renaissance and a new reformation of the human spirit. No great civilization has ever continued to flourish after the loss of its moral and religious convictions and faith.

Finally, it is encouraging to know that out of the crises and periods of trouble in the past have come some of the great experiences and great creative faiths of the race. They can be periods of insight and of growth as well as periods of destruction. Civilization lives and grows through its upward struggles and men tend to strive as they meet obstacles. In biblical times the great periods of moral and religious insight did not come in the times of prosperity, like the reign of Solomon, but in times of trouble like the wilderness and exile experiences. This has been somewhat characteristic of the race as a whole. Out of the wilderness experience came moral insight and new moral codes. Out of the Hebrew exile came a larger view of God, one who was not only the ruler of Palestine, but the Lord of all the nations. He was a God who demanded righteousness and who was revealed in history, in nature, and in man.

Out of these tragic days in which we live may come a keener sense of the moral order of the universe, a realization that men cannot play fast and loose with the laws of wholesome living and escape the penalty. There may come a clearer vision of our need to share the fruits of civilization more fully with all the peoples of the earth. Our horizons, let us hope, may be extended beyond personal and national self-interest, to the need of a world society.

With these elements of encouragement we can face life with a spirit of adventure, with courage, and with faith. Life is a continuous adventure into the unknown. A man's faith ought to be in line with demonstrated possibilities. It may press beyond present facts, but it ought to press forward in the direction in which the facts seem to point. Men must have something to live for or they do not seem to care what they do or whom they follow. There is a trend in evolution, then why not in history and in the lives of men? To run counter to such a trend would mean that life would meet frustration, pain, and extinction. To live in harmony with such a trend would give contentment, peace, and a more abundant life.

FOOTNOTES

Chapter I

1. F. C. Sharp and P. G. Fox, *Business Ethics,* D. Appleton-Century Company, 1937, pp. 3-4.
2. Avis D. Carlson, "Courage for Tomorrow," *Harper's Magazine,* April 1939, Vol. 178, p. 466.
3. *Harper's Magazine,* October 1940, Vol. 181, p. 524.
4. Melvin Rader, *No Compromise,* The Macmillan Company, 1939, p. 293.
5. E. Stanley Jones, *Christ's Alternative to Communism,* Abingdon-Cokesbury Press, 1935, p. 13.
6. W. M. Horton, *Can Christianity Save Civilization,* Harper & Brothers, 1940, p. xi.
7. *Church and State,* Oxford Conference Study Series, Universal Christian Council, 297 Fourth Avenue, New York, p. 3.
8. P. A. Sorokin, *Social and Cultural Dynamics,* 3 Vols., American Book Company, 1937, Vol. 3, *Fluctuation of Social Relationships, War, and Revolution,* p. 535.
9. Albert Schweitzer, *Out of My Life and Thought,* Henry Holt & Company, 1933, trans. by C. T. Campion, p. 279.
10. Albert Schweitzer, *Out of My Life and Thought,* Henry Holt & Company, 1933, trans. by C. T. Campion, p. 281.
11. W. T. Stace, *The Destiny of Western Man,* Reynal & Hitchcock, 1942, p. 189. See also, Lancelot, Hogben, *The Retreat from Reason,* Watts & Co., London, 1936.

Chapter II

1. *Atlantic Monthly,* 166:412.
2. Sumner, W. G., *Folkways,* Ginn & Company, 1911.
3. Stace, W. T., *The Concept of Morals,* The Macmillan Company, 1937, p. 17 ff.
4. Quoted in Dixon, W. Macneile, *The Human Situation,* Longmans, Green & Company, N. D., p. 223.

5. Titus, Harold H., *Ethics for Today,* American Book Company, 1936, p. 449 ff.
6. Hocking, W. E., *Living Religions and a World Faith,* The Macmillan Company, 1940, p. 216.

CHAPTER III

1. See L. T. Hobhouse, *Morals in Evolution,* Henry Holt & Company, Inc., 1923; Edward Westermarck, *The Origin and Development of Moral Ideals,* 2nd ed., Vols. I, II, The Macmillan Company, 1912–1917.
2. Emil Brunner, *The Divine Imperative,* trans. by Olive Wyon, The Macmillan Company, 1937, p. 56.
3. *Romans* 2:14, 15.
4. H. H. Henson, *Christian Morality,* Oxford at the Clarendon Press, 1936, p. 3.

CHAPTER IV

1. Quoted in article by Paul P. Cram, "Undergraduates and the War," *The Atlantic Monthly,* Vol. 166, p. 414.
2. Montague, Wm. Pepperell, *The Ways of Things,* Prentice-Hall, Inc., 1940, pp. 150–151.
3. Stace, W. T., *The Concept of Morals,* The Macmillan Company, 1937, p. 179.
4. Streeter, B. H., *Moral Adventure,* The Macmillan Company, 1929, p. 27 ff.
5. Schweitzer, Albert, *Out of My Life and Thought,* trans. by C. T. Campion, Henry Holt & Company, 1933, p. 254.
6. Quoted in *Federal Council Bulletin,* May 1939, p. 6.
7. *The Madras Series,* Vol. V. *The Economic Basis of the Church,* International Missionary Council, New York, 1939, p. 557.
8. Brown, Harold Chapman, "Ethics from the View Point of Modern Science," *The Journal of Philosophy,* Vol. 34, Mar. 4, 1937, p. 120.
9. *The Madras Series,* Vol. V, *The Economic Basis of the Church,* International Missionary Council, New York, 1939, p. 558.

CHAPTER V

1. Some paragraphs in the following discussion on compromise are taken from, or follow closely, my article, "A Christian Philosophy of Compromise," *The Christian Century,* Nov. 23, 1938.
2. Nicolai Hartmann, *Ethics,* The Macmillan Company, 1932, Vol. 2, *Moral Values,* pp. 281 ff.
3. J. H. Marion, Jr., "Conscience and Circumstance," "The Christian Century," July 16, 1941, p. 908.
4. Dwight J. Bradley, *Social Action,* December 15, 1939, pp. 22–23.
5. Peter Green, *The Problem of Right Conduct,* Longmans, Green, and Company, 1933, pp. 157–158.
6. B. E. Meland, *Write Your Own Ten Commandments,* Willett, Clark, and Company, 1938.
7. Justin Wroe Nixon, *The Moral Crisis in Christianity,* Harper & Brothers, 1931.
8. Ralph W. Sockman, *Morals of Tomorrow,* Harper & Brothers, 1931.
9. B. H. Streeter, *Moral Adventure,* The Macmillan Company, 1939.

CHAPTER VI

1. Jerome Davis, ed., *Labor Speaks for Itself on Religion,* The Macmillan Company, 1929, p. 24.
2. William Clayton Bower, "Education for a New World-Order," in *Religion and the Present Crisis,* ed., by John Knox, University of Chicago Press, 1942, pp. 130–131.
3. *And Who Is My Neighbor,* The Woman's Press, 1929, pp. 17–18.
4. W. G. Sibley, in "Along the Highway," *Chicago Journal of Commerce.*
5. Harry Emerson Fosdick, *The Hope of the World,* Harper & Brothers, 1933, p. 33.
6. H. A. Overstreet, *Our Free Minds,* W. W. Norton & Company, Inc., 1941, pp. 110, 112.

7. Irl Goldwin Whitchurch, *An Enlightened Conscience,* Harper and Brothers, 1941, pp. 241–242.
8. F. Ernest Johnson, *The Church and Society,* The Abingdon-Cokesbury Press, 1934, pp. 221–222.

Chapter VII

1. Hewlett, Johnson, *The Soviet Power,* International Publishers, 1940, p. xiii.
2. Hewlett, Johnson, *The Soviet Power,* International Publishers, 1940, p. 28.
3. See Max Weber, *The Protestant Ethic and the Spirit of Capitalism,* trans. by Talcott Parsons, Charles Scribners & Sons, 1930.
   R. H. Tawney, *The Acquisitive Society,* Harcourt, Brace & Company, Inc., 1920.
   Lewis Mumford, *Faith for Living,* Harcourt, Brace & Company, Inc., 1940, Chapters 22, 23.
4. Archbishop of York, "What Must Christians Do Now?" from *The Christian Century,* October 9, 1940, p. 1242. William Temple, formerly Archbishop of York, became Archbishop of Canterbury April 1, 1942.
5. Quoted by Henry Pitney Van Dusen in *The Christian Century,* Jan. 29, 1941, Vol. 58, p. 146.
6. C. J. Cadoux, *The Journal of Religion,* Vol. XXI, July 1941, p. 239.
7. From Justin Wroe Nixon, *Protestantism's Hour of Decision,* 1940, p. 118, copyright, The Judson Press, Philadelphia. Used by permission.
8. Ware and Means, *The Modern Economy in Action,* Harcourt, Brace & Company, 1936, p. 34.

Chapter VIII

1. Hornell Hart, "Delaware Boiled Down" in *The Christian Century,* August 5, 1942, p. 955. The Delaware Conference was held March 3–5, 1942.
2. Walter W. Van Kirk, *Religion and the World of Tomorrow,* Willett, Clark & Company, 1941, pp. 116–117.

3. *Harper's Magazine,* Vol. 184, pp. 561, 563, May 1942.
4. Quoted in William P. King's *Right and Wrong,* The Abingdon-Cokesbury Press, 1938, p. 20.
5. Chester Rowell, San Francisco *Chronicle,* August 1934.
6. E. Stanley Jones, "The University Christian Mission," *The Christian Century,* January 4, 1939, pp. 10–11.
7. Quoted from a student paper.
8. Harry A. Overstreet, *Our Free Minds,* W. W. Norton & Company, Inc., 1941, p. 135.
9. Arnold J. Toynbee, *A Study of History,* Oxford University Press, 1934, 1939, Vol. IV, pp. 5 ff., Vol. V, pp. 33 ff.

INDEX

Acquisitive society, 72, 134, 173, 217.
Adler, Mortimer J., quoted, 11.
Agar, Herbert, quoted, 201.
Agreements, 106, 109–111.
Altruism, 74 ff.
American youth, 211.
Animal nature or level, 19, 34, 69.
Anthropologists, 31.
Anti-intellectualism, 26, *see also* Retreat from reason.
Apocalyptic ethics, 63.
Aquinas, Thomas, 59–60.
Archbishop of Canterbury, quoted, 177–178.
Aristotle, 48, 70, 88, 95.
Art, 38, 70, 208.
Asceticism, 57, 61, 137.
Atlantic Charter, 199.
Atlantic Monthly, quoted, 30, 77.
Augustine, 58–59.
Authority, authoritarianism, 1, 27, 33, 51, 86, 101, 123 ff., 195.
Aviator, 77.

Barth, Karl, 51, 138.
Behaviorists, 20.
Bentham, Jeremy, 47, 90.
Bible, 10, 33, 51, 52, 63.
Bower, William Clayton, quoted, 134.
Boy Scout movement, 204.
Bradley, Dwight J., quoted, 116–117.
Brown, H. C., quoted, 96.
Brunner, Emil, 51, 138.
Buddhism, 67, 70, 77.
Business, ethics, 6 ff.; business man, 5, 9, 173, 176.
Butler, Joseph, 63.

Cabot, Richard C., 114.
Cadoux, C. J., quoted, 183–184.
Calvin, John, 62.
Campbell, R. J., quoted, 118.
Capitalism, 116, 171, 186, 194, 196.
Carlson, Avis D., quoted, 9.
Chamberlain at Munich, 119.
Change, social, 1 ff., 98 ff.
Character, 86.
Christian, 42, 50, *see also* Jesus Christ, Christianity.
Christian Century, quoted, 177–178, 182, 199–200, 221.
Christian ethics, 43 ff.
Christianity, 43, 157, 216, *see also* Jesus Christ.
Church, 10, 51, 52, 79–80, 133 ff., 156–159.
Civil liberty, 170.
Classical Greeks, 38–39, 46, 64, 67.
Coffin, Henry Sloane, 132.
Communism, 2, 28, 95, 130, 138, 186, 187–188.
Community action, 205–206.
Competition, 186.
Compromise, 106–122.
Confucius, 49, 53, 74.
Conscience, 10, 33, 45, 62–63, 81, 107, 115.
Consequences, 89 ff.
Consumer, 177–178.
Consumers' co-operatives, 2, 175, 186, 188–189.
Corporations, 5, 190.
Courage, 203–204, 218.
Cram, Paul P., 30.
Creative urge, 41.
Crisis, in Western civilization, 1 ff., 23, 170, 192–218.

225

Crisis theology, 51, 63, 138.
Cross, 75–76, 140–141.
Customs, customary morality, 10, 36–37, 44 ff., 76, 121.

Darwin, Charles, 20.
Davis, Jerome, 221.
Dean of Canterbury, quoted, 171.
Delaware conference, on peace, 190, 199–200.
Democracy, 3, 12, 27, 162–168, 197.
Development, of Morality and ethics, 44–50, 101.
Dewey, John, 70.
Dictatorship, 20, 26, 72, *see also* Fascism.
Discipline, 84, 88.
Dixon, W. Macneile, quoted, 35, 219.
Doctor, medical, 5, 9.
Duty, in Kant, 46–47; Jesus on, 54–55; to God, 102 ff.
Dynamic, morality as, 65, 68, 101–102.

East versus west, 49.
Economic relationships, 73, 168–178.
Edinburgh, conference, 80, 197.
Education, 1, 209, *see also* Specialists.
Emotions, 40, 85, 98 ff., 149–152, 206.
Employers, employees, 5.
Encouragement, grounds for, 214–218.
Ends or goals, 47 ff., 52, 68 ff.
Equality, 78.
Erskine, John, 81.
Escape, religion as a means of, 137 ff.; from reality, 203.
Ethical relativism, 21, 24, 29–33.
Ethics of Jesus, 52 ff.
Evangelism, 92 ff.
Exceptions, *see* Compromise.
Experimentation, in morality, 106, 123–129, 175.

Faith, 218.
Family, 75, 77.
Farmer, 173, 176.
Fascism, 2, 20, 24–29, 131, 172, 186, 187, 194, 197, 198, 200.
Federal Council of Churches, 190, 199.
Fellowship, 70, 72–73, 80.
Feudal society, 50.
Fichte, 71.
First world war, 3, 4, 21, 82, 83, 181, 199, 200.
Forgiveness, 148.
Formalism, 46–47, 64.
Fosdick, Harry Emerson, quoted, 141–142.
Freedom, 5, 20, 70, 86, 162, 170, 198.
Freudians, 20.
Functional society, 73; ethics, 64.
Fundamentalism, 50, 63.

Gentile, G., 26.
God, 28, 42, 51–56, 63, 75, 104–105, 130, 138, 145–149, 152, 155–156, 216.
Golden rule, 74.
Good, 66, 68 ff., 81.
Green, Canon Peter, quoted, 117.
Green, T. H., 70, 86–87.
Group action, 204–206.
Growth, 98 ff., 153–155, 210–214.
Guilt, for war, 200–201.

Happiness, 11, 38, 47, 79, 202.
Harper's Magazine, quoted, 9, 11–12, 201.
Hart, Hornell, quoted, 199–200.
Hartmann, Nicolai, quoted, 115.
Hatred, 198–199.
Hebrew prophets, 53, 64, 87, 143–144.
Hedonism, 47, *see also* Utilitarianism, Happiness.
Hegel, 70.
Henson, H. H., quoted, 63.
Hinduism, 49.
Hitler, 25, 194, 195, 200, 201.

Hobhouse, L. T., 220.
Hocking, W. E., quoted, 41–42.
Honesty, 38, 109–110, 113–115.
Honor, 109, *see also* Honesty.
Horton, W. M., quoted, 14–15.
Humanists, 70, 103.
Humanitarianism, 3, 25.
Human nature, 34 ff., 63, 75, 80–81, 95.

Ideals, 120–121, 147, 210–214.
Individualism, 4, 62, 171, 186–187.
Industrial revolution, 18, 161, 169 ff.
In-group, 79.
Inner controls, 86 ff.
Institutionalism, 134–137.
Intelligence, 80 ff.; in religion, 151–152.
Interim ethics, 55.
International relations, 3, 25, 76, 119, 177–186, 206.
Intuitionism, 46–47.
Irrationalism, 26, 37, *see also* Retreat from reason.
Islam, 49, 67.
Isolation, 201.

Jesus, Jesus Christ; ethics of, 52 ff., 42, 70, 87–88, 97, 104–105, 107, 122, 128, 140–141, 149, 152, 185, 186.
Jews, 26, 54, 77.
Johnson, F. Ernest, quoted, 159; 222.
Johnson, Hewlett, quoted, 171.
Jones, E. Stanley, quoted, 13, 211.
Judgment of God, 201.
Justice, 75; social, 160 ff.
Justin Martyr, 56–57.

Kant, Immanuel, 46–47, 55, 70, 88, 89–90.
Kingdom of God, 164.
King, W. P., 223.
Knowledge, 39–40, 80 ff., 207.

Labor, 132; espionage, 53; Unions, 5, 53, 117.
Laissez-faire, 4, 62, 171, 186–187.
Lao-tze, 49.
Law, 36, 45 ff., 76, 121.
Lawyer, 6.
League of Nations, 53, 120, 177, 181, 194, 197, 201.
Lester, Muriel, 82.
Logical positivism, 30.
Love, 35, 55, 74 ff.
Loyalty, 55, 66.
Luther, Martin, 61, 145.

Madras conference, 80, 197; quoted, 94, 97.
Man, 34 ff., 147.
Marion, J. H. Jr., quoted, 115–117.
Marriage, 129.
McCown, C. C., 55.
McGovern, 195.
Means, moral, 89 ff.
Medieval period, 59, 62.
Meland, B. E., 125–126.
Meliorism, 164, 213.
Militarism, 25, 28, *see also* War.
Mill, John Stuart, 47, 90.
Minority, 32, 216.
Moderation, 67.
Mohammedan, 49, 67.
Monopoly, 170, 174.
Montague, W. P., quoted, 77–78.
Moore, G. E., 70.
Moral objectivity, 31–32.
Moral order of universe, 201, 217.
Motives, 66, 89 ff.
Mumford, Lewis, 3.
Mussolini, 24 ff., 194, 195.

Nationalism, 3, 25, 77, 200.
National Socialism, 24–29, *see also* Fascism.
Natural law, 11, 57, 62.
Naturalism, 30.
Nature, 11, 34, 48, 63.
Nature of morality, 33 ff.
Negroes, 115–116, 136–137.
Neo-Supernaturalism, 138–139.

New Testament, 64–65, 144.
Nietzsche, 20.
Nixon, Justin Wroe, 126.
Nonviolence, 159, 185.

Obedience, 50.
Objective, objectivity, 29, 48, 83, 208.
Old Testament, 144, 152.
Opportunism, 26–27.
Origen, 57.
Orthodox, 50, 77.
Overstreet, Harry A., quoted, 142; 213.
Oxford conference, quoted, 14; 80, 19'.

Pacifism, 181–186, *see also* Peace.
Page, Kirby, quoted, 143.
Paul, the Apostle, 56, 88, 122, 148–149.
Peace, 25, 119, 166, 178–186, 199–200.
Personal preference, 10.
Persons, personality, 68–73, 104.
Philosophical ethics, 46 ff., 51, 57, 65, 67.
Philosophy, 38–39, 53, 70, 208.
Physical level of life, 19, 34, 69, 210.
Planning, 95, *see also* Chapter VII.
Plato, 38–39, 48, 59, 70, 84, 95.
Politics, 72, 118.
Poverty, 8, 169.
Private enterprise, 173, 186.
Privilege, 170.
Professions, 6.
Profit motive, 178–179, 186.
Progress, 12, 17, 22, 101–102, 107–108, 128, 169, 209.
Property, 72, 118, 174, 186.
Protestantism, 60, 132, 145.
Protestant Reformation, 60 ff., 101, 123, 130, 144–145.
Psychology, 30, 37, 53.
Punishment, 145, 148.
Puritans, 24, 62.

Race, racial prejudice, 26–28, 77, 168; racial progress, 115–116.
Rader, Melvin, quoted, 13.
Rationalization, 99, *see also* Self-deceit.
Rauschning, Hermann, 28.
Reader's Digest, 204.
Reason, 38–39, 63, *see also* Intelligence, Reflective morality.
Reflective morality, 39 ff., 45 ff., 69, 203 ff.
Regionalism, 201–202.
Religion, 23, 38, 64, 70, 102–106, 130–159, 208, 210; ethical, 149–156; unethical, 132–149.
Religious sects, 139.
Remnant, 216.
Renaissance, 20, 101, 123, 130.
Responsibility, 44, 54, 192–218.
Retreat from reason, 19, 206.
Revolution, 21, 197, *see also* Crisis, Industrial revolution.
Rights, 44, 55, 68 ff.
Roman Catholicism, 60.
Rowell, Chester, quoted, 206–207.
Royden, Maude, quoted, 201.
Rules, 68, 111–113.

Sabbath Day, 71.
Salvation, 145–149.
Schleiermacher, 150.
Scholasticism, 59–60.
Schopenhauer, 20.
Science, and scientists, 1, 18–19, 38–39, 41, 70, 83, 207–210.
Schweitzer, Albert, quoted, 17; 54, 84.
Second world war, 21, 199, 200, 201, *see also* War.
Sectarianism, 134–137.
Secularism, 133 ff., 200, 217.
Self, 68–73, 104.
Self-control, 67.
Self-deceit, 109–110, 150.
Self-denial, 74 ff.
Self-interest, 4, 8, 72, 95, 119, 170.
Selfishness, 23, 38, 78–79.
Selflessness, 74 ff.

Self-realization, 48–49, 64.
Self-sacrifice, 74 ff.
Separation, of religion and morality, 8, 22–23, 139–150; of science and morality, 208–210.
Shakespeare, 29, 141.
Sharp, F. C. and Fox P. Q., quoted, 6–7; 219.
Shaw, G. B., 6.
Shotwell, James T., 199.
Sin, 56, 67, 145–149, 172.
Skeptics, 32–33, 42.
Social change, 1 ff., 159, 164 ff.
Social gospel, 92 ff, 158.
Social level, of life, 36 ff.
Socialism, 2, 186, 188.
Social reconstruction, 92 ff.
Social welfare, 11, 46, 158.
Sockman, Ralph W., quoted, 126.
Socrates, 70.
Sorokin, P. A., quoted, 15.
Sovereignty, 119, 179–180.
Specialists and specialization, 20, 83, 207–210.
Spencer, Herbert, 13, 48.
Spengler, Oswald, 14–15, 17.
Stace, W. T., 31; quoted, 78.
State, 25, 28, *see also* Democracy.
Stoicism, 70.
Streeter, B. H., 81, 126.
Student, quoted, 211–212.
Subjectivism, 29, 31–32, 48.
Sumner, W. G., 31.
Sympathy, 40, 74 ff., 205.

Tawney, R. H., 222.
Teacher, 6, *see also* Education, Specialists.
Teleological approach in ethics, 47 ff.
Temple, William, quoted, 177–178, 222.
Tolerance, 207.
Tolstoy, 63.
Totalitarianism, *see* Fascism.
Toynbee, Arnold, 15–17, 216–217.

Traditionalism, 26.
Trends in civilization, 12 ff.
Tribalism, 134–137.
Truthfulness, 113–115.

Undergraduates, and the war, 29–30, 211–212.
Union Now, 53.
Universalism, in morality, 54.
Unselfishness, 38–40, 74 ff.
Utilitarianism, 47, 64, 70, 90.

Values, 68 ff., 110, 192 ff., 209.
Van Dusen, Henry P., quoted, 182.
Van Kirk, Walter W., 200; quoted, 201.
Versailles, treaty, 194.
Vicarious sacrifice, 140–141.
Vices, 38, 56.
Virtues, 38, 56, 172.
Voltaire, 82.

War, 2, 20–21, 28, 119, 166, 177–186, 196–201, *see also* First world war, Second world war.
Ware and Means, quoted, 187.
Wealth, 72.
Weber, Max, 222.
Weiss, Johannes, 54.
Westermarck, 31.
Western civilization, 1, 12 ff., 28, 30, 43, 49, 61, 123, 165, 192 ff., 204, 217.
Whale, John S., quoted, 93–94.
Whitchurch, I. G., quoted, 142–143.
Whitehead, A. N., 2.
Will of God, 10, 51, 91.
Will-to-live, 34 ff., 210.
World Court, 120, 197, 201.
World federation, 177, 199–200.
Worship, 205.
Worth of persons, 67–73.

Youth, 211.

Zoroastrianism, 49.

Φ

R/N 79BKCA
TITUS